Copyright © 2019 by

All rights reserved. No part of this book may be reproduced, stored in a retrieval system, or transmitted in any form or by any means, electronic, mechanical, photocopying, recording, scanning, or otherwise, without the prior written permission of the publisher.

Disclaimer

All the material contained in this book is provided for educational and informational purposes only. No responsibility can be taken for any results or outcomes resulting from the use of this material.

While every attempt has been made to provide information that is both accurate and effective, the author does not assume any responsibility for the accuracy or use/misuse of this information.

Some names have been changed and/or omitted in order to protect the privacy of certain characters in this book.

TABLE OF CONTENTS

INTRODUCTION 1

CHAPTER ONE: START SMALL 10

CHAPTER TWO: FINANCE 21

CHAPTER THREE: SOURCING FOR ADVICE .. 31

CHAPTER FOUR: PROFESSIONAL PROPERTY ASSESSMENT 44

CHAPTER FIVE: DOCUMENTATION AND PROPERTY MANAGEMENT 55

CHAPTER SIX: CONSIDERING ECONOMIC AND RENTAL VALUE 69

CHAPTER SEVEN: MARKETING AND ADVERTISING 85

CHAPTER EIGHT: KNOW YOUR TARGET RENTER 103

CHAPTER NINE: HOLIDAY/ VACATION RENTAL INVESTMENT 124

CHAPTER TEN: NATIONAL AND
INTERNATIONAL PROPERTY 144

CONCLUSION 165

INTRODUCTION

Real estate is the real deal for many individuals. Unfortunately, a lot of people have failed to recognize the advantages of real estate investment and are concerned with the risk associated with real estate. Yes, there are risks in real estate! Is there any profit without incurring a loss?

Inasmuch as there are risks associated with real estate investment, it doesn't stop it from being a profitable business venture and a good way to make passive income. Real estate investment can be narrowed down to owning rental property. This aspect of real estate investment is uncommon in society because a lot of people do not recognize the advantages of such a business venture.

A look at society today reveals a vacuum that needs to be filled. One important fact to bear in mind is that real estate investment will never depreciate. It survives the test of time, and this is one advantage that other business ventures cannot guarantee.

Owning rental property is an aspect of real estate investment that involves purchasing a property and putting it up for lease. In this form of business investment, an individual purchases a rental property and makes decisions on how best to utilize the property. In most cases, the individual who owns the rental property may decide either to put it up for lease or resell it to another interested buyer. Any of the following options is profitable to the person who owns the rental property.

The major problems associated with owning a rental property are managing the property and dealing with the tenants. Just like the name, "rental property" reveals that the property was formerly in use before another interested buyer purchased it. This implies there would be a great deal of repair on such property. As such, it requires a reasonable amount of capital to manage the repairs and put the property in an admirable state. Whether the end goal is to put up the property for lease or to sell the property, the fact remains that no one will be willing to pay for a house that is in a bad shape. So, to avert such unwanted circumstances, it is important to take care of putting the property in good working condition. Unfortunately, a lot of people do not want to incur additional cost on a property after purchasing it. So, this is a major factor that discourages people from owning rental property.

Another problem is in dealing with tenants. Undoubtedly, there are good tenants who would be ready to cooperate and ensure there is little friction between the landlord and the tenants. But, this is not always the case. Tenants are sometimes a handful to deal with, and some very crafty tenants bring up all sort of trick to avoid paying rent on your property. Many times, it doesn't end well for the individual who owns the property, as he bears the burden of forcefully collecting rent from such tenants. This problem makes owning rental properties seem like a bad investment.

The presence of all these problems is not enough to rule out the benefits of owning real rental property. The good news is that there are ways to handle the problems effectively and make passive income out of the property.

An effective way of handling these problems is to have a good strategy of acquiring a rental property. The right way to go about owning rental property is to survey the property to be bought carefully. If this is too much for you to handle, then engage the services of a professional who would assist in surveying the property. The reason behind the survey is to determine if owning the rental property would be a good investment. It would be a bad investment if you spend more money on repairs than on the actual cost of the property. The real estate agents are also in the right position to offer professional advice on issues revolving around owning rental property. More so, in surveying the rental property, you also bear your financial strength in mind, and this would avert circumstances where you may not be able to manage the property after owning it.

Tenants are quite worrisome, especially the difficult tenants who are concerned with frustrating your efforts as a landlord. The good news is that you don't have to deal with them directly. One question that plagues the heart of individuals who want to own rental property is: "How do I collect my rent from difficult tenants?" As a matter of fact, you do not need to deal with tenants directly. Employ the services of a property manager. The property manager would be the intermediary between the tenants and the landlord. In this way, you don't deal with them directly and won't be caught up in a web of emotions. Now you see, it isn't as difficult as it seems!

The benefits of owning rental properties are tremendous and, as such, reveal how exciting and profitable the investment is. A good way to make additional money is by owning rental properties. This would seem like a surprise to many, considering some inevitable factors such as financial involvement. Owning rental property is a means of generating a passive source of income. This implies that, as the landlord or owner of the property, you can get engaged in other professional activities and still generate money by putting up the house for lease.

Alternatively, owning rental properties provides a sense of security. In cases where the rental property was bequeathed to you and you do not want to give it up for sale, the option at your disposal is to put it up for rent. By so doing, you are assured the property will not be at the risk of abandonment, which may affect its state and living condition.

Additionally, owning rental property comes with the option of the flexibility of sale. If at any point the owner of the rental property decides to sell the property, it is easier to sell at a reasonable price because the landlord must have made some money out of its rent. Thus, selling the property would not incur loss but rather bring in more profits. More so, the property would appreciate over time, and its value would increase as the demand for shelter increases among the population. So, the landlord is in the position to decide the best time to give out the house.

There is a possibility that, as the owner of rental property, you may decide to make use of that property for personal reasons. This could be a result of work-related reasons or as a temporary residence. Rather than go through the hurdles of paying rent at another property, you can make use of your property and save a good amount of money.

A quick survey of the American population reveals that people prefer to rent properties. A good number of individuals in their teens and young adult life have resorted to renting properties rather than purchasing properties. In the past ten years, the number of people who rent homes has skyrocketed, and this had made the rental market wax stronger by the day. This is because many Americans are comfortable with the flexibility of rental homes rather than owning homes.

The relevance of owning properties dwindled in 2004, and this has paved a way for rental properties to survive.

In all, owning rental property minimizes your susceptibility to risk-prone factors, such as financial embarrassment, homelessness, and security-related problems.

Every financially dependent individual is expected to own a rental property and make the best use of it. Times are changing, and things are changing with it. To prevent unpleasant circumstances associated with the failure to make adequate plans, it is expected that people invest in owning rental properties. The risk is minimal and can be adequately controlled or even totally prevented if the right measures are taken. Another notable factor is that, as the owner of a rental property, you can decide not to be directly involved with the property management and still get good returns from the property.

What else are you worried about? Absolutely nothing! Rather than bother with factors that are almost non-existent, look at the numerous advantages of the investment and make proper use of the property.

All the information you seek will be made known to you in the course of this article. As a matter of fact, this article is an inspiring work that will reveal a lot of hidden secrets to owning rental properties, as well as the trick behind managing the property successfully and getting the very best out of it. Take a ride with me!

CHAPTER ONE

START SMALL

Owning rental properties is a good means to generate money. It is extremely important that you go about it the proper way. One pertinent thing to bear in mind before commencing with the plan to venture into the business is that the results may not be as fast as you desire. It is a profitable business, but it requires patience and dedication to see the business grow and blossom.

If you are desirous of making investment properties, rental properties are the best plan for you to favor. It is an investment that assures you of a reliable source of income. Unlike the belief of so many people, in the real estate investment structure, it is more of profits and fewer losses.

Although it doesn't totally rule out the place of losses with the right guidance, you are sure to get the best off your property. In owning a rental property, it is best to settle for small properties. As a first-time investor, you need to understand the place of baby steps. You barely understand the market structure and the risks involved in the business. Therefore, it is erroneous to make hasty plans and conclusions about the market.

This business structure is capital intensive. It requires a lot of finances because there are certain areas that would require to be taken care of. The simple trick to excelling in the rental property business is to start very small. Starting small has many benefits. These benefits stem from the fact that, as a first- time investor, it reduces the amount of finance that would be required in maintaining the property. More so, you may not fully have the capacity to handle the issues involved in large commercial properties.

What type of mind-set do you have for the business? It won't be a surprise if you have doubts. But, you need to eliminate every trace of doubt in your heart and accept the possibilities of growing the business. Listen, no one said it will be easy, but it will surely be worth it. You need to be available mentally, physically, and emotionally to excel in a rental property business venture. Your expectation from the property will influence the choices you make. You need to understand the duration it may take. Knowing that rental property is a quick way to make money doesn't explain that it will be an easy process. As a matter of fact, it will not be easy to make the investment and realize the kind of money you have anticipated. In all, your expectation should never waver. It may take time, but it will be achieved with consistency and determination. To attain that height, you need to understand that it will be a gradual process.

There are numerous individuals who venture into owning rental properties because they desire having an influential lifestyle or want to get rich quickly from such property. All of it is possible, but you must maintain your initial goal of having the property establishment.

Sustaining your investment is solely dependent on how you begin. A first-time investor who is governed by the get-rich-quick syndrome doesn't really excel in owning rental property. This is because such investors usually expect too much return from the investment and even over-exaggerate the returns. Such a mind-set in this business venture is bound to be crowned by the ultimate failure of the business venture. To excel in owning rental properties, you need to set some realistic goals. Your goals and expectations should be real and not overly exaggerated. The truth is you can't recover all the money you spent on the property in the first year. It could take longer than planned. This is one of the reasons first-time investors are greatly advised to take things easy and start on a small scale. Set your priorities right, so you don't get disappointed after the first few months!

The right way to go about this is to invest in single dwelling places. Single dwelling places reduce the stress involved in taking care of the property. In this way, you have fewer tenants on your property; as such, it is easier to collect your rent. Additionally, there would be minimal repairs to be done on the property. A larger property presupposes a lot of wear and tear, and you will be saddled with the responsibility of keeping the property fit to be rented out to willing individuals.

Beginning small by using single-family dwellings provides the necessary skill you will require as a landlord. You need to understand how the market functions. It would give you insight to functioning well in the real estate sector. At the end of the day, your major desire is to widen your scope and engage more in having bigger properties and investment, but you won't do too well in this field unless you gain the necessary experience. Undeniably, there are options for engaging the services of a property manager. But, no property manager will handle your property the way you would. There is always a difference between a property manager and the owner of the property. The property manager is the intermediary between the tenants and the landlord. He may not fully understand the importance of the property the way you would handle the property. As a property owner, you are driven by the sense of responsibility, and as such, you will handle the property like a suitable business venture.

No matter how hard people try to conceal the truth, the real state of the situation is that you need to get involved in the affairs of your property. Do not entrust the care of your property to a third party who may not fully understand how you got to acquire the property. For this reason, it is right for investors who are new in the real situation of things to start small and then grow over time.

As a first-time investor who acquires a single-family dwelling, you are more involved in the affairs of your property, and this would provide you with the experience to make the property better and to your expected standard. In a single-family dwelling, it is easier for you to attend to repairs on the property promptly.

It is also pertinent that first-time investors work according to their budget. In the choice of property, ensure you acquire or purchase properties that are similar to your previous experiences. As a potential investor who wants to invest in owning rental properties, you had been staying on another person's property before making the decision to get yours. What were your experiences? There would be certain things you must have experienced on the property where you once lived. Take that experience and inculcate it into what you intend on starting. Your previous experiences are a necessary stepping stone to ensure you derive optimum satisfaction from the rental property you hope to acquire.

Another aspect to starting small is to consider the vicinity where you want to acquire a property. This is very important in making an investment. You need to understand the place of getting a suitable environment where your investment would appreciate over time. If you fail to pick a location you are conversant with, you may not realize the adverse effects on such choice you have made. Familiarity with an environment helps you to understand all there is to the environment. If there are factors that are life-threatening or exposed to environmental hazards, you would be aware. It is essential for you to understand how to get a suitable location. The best thing to settle for is a location that is very close to you. Get a location that you can access. Proximity should be very important to you. Any location you cannot get easy access to can cause trouble or future problems for you. So, you need to avoid it at all cost.

A common mistake many first-time investors make is that they fail to understand the risks attached to a certain location and make the investment without asking appropriate questions. The first step to take is to conduct research on your choice of property. Your choice of environment must be guided by questions such as: "What do I hope to benefit from my property in this location?" "In the nearest future, what is the hope of my property on this location?" These questions must be adequately answered if you really want to go on with such an environment. Investing in a rental property is not done by sentiments. No, you need to understand what you are going into and, as such, attach a high level of importance to it.

You also need to need to weigh the consequences of your actions. If you are settling for an environment where you barely understand the elements at play in such vicinity, be prepared to accept whatever negative thing comes out from it. Will the efforts and the resources invested in such place be worth your effort? Is it a profitable business venture? How much rent can you realize from such an environment? These questions can only be answered after you have conducted your research.

The only guarantee with owning a rental property is that it provides a passive source of income for you and doesn't interfere with your personal lifestyle and professional life. Who wouldn't want some extra bucks? Of course, everyone does! This doesn't rule out the effects of expecting too much. Most times, you only get disappointed when you have expected too much. When you don't, you are never disappointed. So, to avert later regrets and disappointments, have a proper plan and work according to what you can afford. Don't be in a hurry to expect the best of your property. Allow things to fall into their right place, but you must be willing to start small.

The primary purpose of owning the property is to generate money from individuals who would be willing to pay rent on your property. Hence, it is important to consider the interest of your tenants as well. Quite a number of persons love an apartment that allows for outdoor services. It could be as little as a garden space. But whatever the case, you need to ensure your property is going to have an attractive shape. Rental properties are a bit competitive now, unlike how it was some years ago. Too many persons are now interested in renting a home rather than owning a home because renting permits a flexible way of living. So, to stand out among the competitors, get something renters desire, an apartment that guarantees privacy as well as security. More so, your tenants won't be willing to pay too much on maintenance. So, it is important to make the right decisions to save cost for yourself and your tenants.

It is very important to consider your intentions for the property and make decisions that affect your choice positively.

******

CHAPTER TWO

FINANCE

This is a prerequisite step in getting involved with an investment of any sort. Any individual can desire to own a rental property, but not everyone is financially responsible to take up what the project entails.

The first question to ask is: "How much do I intend to spend on a property?" You need to have a budget and expect to work with the budget. It is wrong to expect to own a property without prior understanding of the capital involvement of such a project. It is a good idea to own rental property, as it provides for a passive source of income. But, it is also considered a careless decision if the odds are not taken into consideration. No matter how attractive a property looks on the outside, never be too quick to come to hasty conclusions about purchasing or owning that property.

Owning rental property involves a lot of financial commitment. An important factor to recognize when owning rental property is the fact that rental property comes with a lot of financial burden. There may be a need for some repairs on the property, and the one in charge of the property is saddled with the responsibility if ensuring the property is in good condition. It is always best to consult or engage the services of a financial expert to provide professional advice that would make the process less tedious.

Financial experts are equipped with the right information regarding sourcing money for making an investment. As a matter of fact, there are a lot of available options at your disposal. Unless you consult a financial expert, you may never know of such options.

One of the many options available is making use of a **mortgage** to own the rental property. A Mortgage is actually a good way to own rental property because it minimizes the cost of acquiring the rental property. However, it is also right to point out that there are actually some pitfalls to this option. Using a mortgage as leverage to own property can actually incur additional costs and expenses for the person who has acquired the rental property. In the course of owning a property, there will be a need for repairs and other unforeseen damages on the properties. The burden of this repair is solely that of the individual who has acquired the property. You also need to have an understanding of how long the mortgage plan will last. Is it going to be a flexible mortgage plan? What does it involve? It is important to weigh the cost of the option and decide if it is the right financing option for you. Now, it is obvious that there are some advantages and disadvantages of using a mortgage as leverage to own properties. So, it is important to seek professional advice from a financial expert to make the right financial decision.

No one likes a bad investment, and the only factor that makes an investment look bad is inadequate planning. It is not enough to make a decision to own rental property. It is also best to consider your financial strength. Some individuals prefer to **save up money** and then use it towards acquiring properties. It is actually a good alternative, provided the individual who is interested in the property is financially able to handle the property and what it entails.

Another available option for individuals who are sourcing finance to own rental properties is to seek help **online**. There are a number of online financial experts who are willing to give a loan on a considerable interest rate. All a potential investor needs to do is understand how to get in touch with those online sites, fill the basic information, and follow the due process to hasten the process. A good example of an online platform is Lendingtree. This platform provides access for potential investors to seek help online. In this way, it exposes the potential investor to a number of multiple lenders who would be in competition for the loan and helps you find a suitable fit.

It is usually the most difficult for first-time investors. Older investors have the basic idea of how to source loans, unlike new investors who are still struggling to get a grasp of what real estate entails. If it is your first time investing in rental property, do not get carried away with the excitement of being a landlord. Rather, pay attention to what being a landlord involves. The financing aspect of an investment is sacrosanct because it can either make or break the intent behind the investment. A single financial mistake can bring the whole project to ruins and leave you nowhere. To avert such circumstances, it is necessary to weigh different options available at your disposal.

There is always a multitude of people who are willing to help, provided you seek the right counsel. Another option of sourcing finance to begin your project is from the **seller of the property.** How? The seller of the property is the individual who is willing to transfer the ownership of his property to you for a considerable amount of money. The right way to go about this is to ask the seller to loan you some money. Yes, you heard correctly! The seller of the property can actually help finance your dreams of owning a property! It is really a better option than seeking loans from the bank. The seller of the property can actually be another property investor or a person who lives on the property. You can ask the seller to assist you with the down payment of the property or even the full cost of the property.

The best way to secure this agreement between both parties is to make it legal. You and the seller who is financing the property cost must reach an agreement, which would be duly signed by the parties involved. This is necessary to prevent chances of future disagreement, which can put your ownership of the property at stake.

Alternatively, you can decide to settle for a **partnership-based ownership** of the rental property. What this simply means is that you can get a passive party involved in your investment plans. There is absolutely nothing wrong with asking for help from a friend who you know is financially capable to assist you to finance the project. You could ask help from a close family member or friend who has the necessary resources but doesn't want to get directly involved in managing the property. This financing option allows you to run the affairs of the property while the other person pays the cost of owning the property. Now, you and your partner will need to come to an agreement on how the proceeds realized from the rental property will be shared. What matters is that, at the end of the day, you and your partner make profits from the property.

This ensures that you and your partner share equal risk in owning the property. That is, your partner bears the financial risk of the investment while you bear the risk of managing the property and seeing it yield profitable returns. Nonetheless, the profits realized will be shared according to the kind of effort both partners have contributed. The agreement reached by both parties must be documented and signed by both parties.

Another financing option is to encourage the presence of **government loans.** Government loans can also be used to finance owning rental properties. A lot of people do not like to make use of government loans because they conclude that the laws governing the use of loans are stringent and difficult to abide by. The veiled reality is that government loans are the best options for individuals who are investing in rental properties for the first time.

The FHA, otherwise known as the Federal Housing Administration, is a government scheme that is programmed to help people own their own properties with a minimal percentage, which will be paid as the down payment. These loans are considered the best financing options for owning rental properties because they are cost-effective. The way government loans are given out varies from one country to the next. This implies that different countries have their loan limit. The trick behind this is that the potential investor is privileged to utilize the opportunity and request a loan to buy a multi-property. The more units in a rental property, the more rent that is accrued for the landlord.

The last available option is to make use of your **retirement account**. It is not a good idea to retire and leave yourself destitute. Owning a rental property makes life easier when you are much older. Rather than be at the mercy of the banks for loans or seek the help of an individual who may not be willing to buy into your dreams and investment plans, you can decide to make use of your retirement account to own a rental property. But, to make this a reality, there is a need to consult with your CPA who is most likely in the best position to provide the necessary details and how you can go about it. Though, before you commence with this option, you must be ready to put in the needed energy and time to pull the investment through.

Investing in owning rental properties is a lucrative investment, considering the fact that it comes with some financial benefits. These benefits stem from the fact that it enables you to generate a passive income from the property while getting involved in another business venture. Nonetheless, it is important to apply caution while dealing with the available financial options. Before settling for any financial option, be sure to understand the pros and cons of the options you have chosen. The keyword is to be very observant and careful in all your dealings. Never forget to talk to people who are seasoned professionals in the financial industry. The necessary details to bear in mind are the importance of having an agreement duly signed by the parties involved, a legal document that would specify how the proceeds will be shared by the different partners, and your projections of how much would be realized from owning the rental property. This would give you an insight into determining if the rental property is a worthy investment.

*****

CHAPTER THREE

SOURCING FOR ADVICE

Property investment is an ever-changing commitment, and you need to keep up with challenges and trends. It is no news that real estate has empowered many, even the world's wealthiest persons, so it's a great idea to believe that property is a wise investment. Like every other investment package, without the proper know-how, you are heading for a big downfall, which is why it is advisable to ask questions and do research when and where possible.

The big question now is who to go to and what sort of questions to ask in regard to rental property investment. The question of who is quite simple; real estate is all about relationships, right connections, and good reputations. Meet with every person you can, as there is no one not worth your time. Your best bets are estate agents, landlords, property sourcing companies, developers and resourceful books { don't forget reading is a large part of the research process} to mention but a few. You should build a trust-based relationship with them over a period of time.

Try attending property investment seminars once in a while to gain valuable insights and build a peer network {peers can provide mutual support and guidance}, join a local association of landlords and get up-to-date information, speak to people to let them know you're looking to buy a property. These and many more are the various people/gatherings you can talk to/visit for vital information before going for that investment. The problem is, until you start getting and gaining experience, no one is going to take your intentions seriously.

Moving on to what sorts of questions to ask when you're in contact with any of the avenues mentioned above, these questions will be highlighted in this chapter, and possible answers will be provided to make your research flexible.

QUESTIONS TO CONSIDER ASKING YOUR SOURCE

You want to venture into the real estate business and become a tycoon in the long run? Before you dive into property investment with thousands of dollars, try equipping yourself with vital information such as:

- **Understand why you want to do this.**

    One question you might be asked is the question of WHY? Before you answer, ask yourself if this is actually for you. Are you a handyman? Can you take the heat of paperwork and tenant issues? What about the issues of tax and mortgage? Are you buying to own a property as an investment or a source of income? These and many more are questions you should ask yourself before you're asked.

- **Are you financially sound?**

    Another crucial factor to consider is your financial strength if you want to get in and stay in. Avoid debts at all cost; don't carry it as part of your investment portfolio. If you have outstanding bills, such as medical, student loans, and the like, purchasing a rental property may not be the right move. Just so you know, investment properties generally require a down payment, so don't put yourself in a position where you lack the means to make payments. Perhaps you're thinking of borrowing money; remember the cost of borrowing might be cheap, but the interest rate on an investment property would be on the high part. Always have a margin of safety.

- **Your cash flow agenda**

Now that you know why you want to do this and your financial strength, let's discuss how to make the cash flow in. A rental purchase should have an interesting cash flow and good rate of return. Be sure to ask your agent how much profit you should make on a rental property because, as soon as you are aware of the factors at play in the purchase of your property, it would give you insight into how much you will rent out your property. It is advisable to start with an affordable investment, like a single unit or a duplex, rather than a whole apartment building because the more expensive the home, the higher the ongoing expenses will be.

Avoid properties that require major repairs; they could cost you more than your budget. To keep the cash flowing, don't spend too much upgrading a rental property. That's why you have tenants- you can inform your tenants to pay a certain amount monthly to handle repairs when the need arises. An important thing is to consider what type of maintenance is required based on your property purchase. Imagine you purchase a townhouse. The maintenance is included in the initial fee, which means any repairs that come along fall on you. This cannot be compared to a single-family home; the landlord is generally responsible for little things, like lawn mowing or snow removal.

For every dollar you invest, you should be able to account for your return. Be sure to ask your agents about the details.

- **How much of a handy-man are you?**

Remember this was asked in your 'Why you want to do this?' question. If you're not buoyant enough to get an agent to oversee your property, then you need to be ready to do a whole lot of work. A landlord has a lot to deal with, paperwork, late rent, loud tenants, and the likes. It is advisable to choose your tenants wisely. Nobody wants a tenant that signifies trouble because dealing with one can be stressful. You have to be prepared to screen your tenants carefully and thoroughly to avoid being caught in a difficult tenant situation. You need to develop a tough skin. Investing in rental property is not for the faint-hearted.

As a landlord, do you know your way around basic home repairs? Perhaps a little knowledge in carpentry or plumbing? It is an advantage for property owners to do their own basic repairs to save cost. If you can't take up these responsibilities, then you hire an agent to get them done, but it will cost you.

- **Find a profit-centered rental property.**

  In finding a property, it's not about the cheapest but the economic factors. First is your location. This is one of the most important things when purchasing a rental property. Pick a great location with good infrastructure, as this would make the area attractive to renters. There should be easy access to transit/major roads, schools, shopping malls, recreation, and so on, as this would make a huge difference. In addition, is the society developing? Is it making adequate provisions for individuals and jobs? What is their crime rate? Note that a community on the rise has a good chance of attracting profitable rent and an increase in the value of a rental property. Remember to ask, in detail, how all these work when you are making further research.

On a final note, every financial decision or commitment is about taking a risk. You weigh your rewards and losses, but the good news is, in rentals, your income is passive. Although tenants may prove difficult, you can always hire an agent or use a property management company.

It is important to seek help when you realize that you cannot do it all alone. You need to seek help from the right kind of individuals. There are no other persons to provide the best kind of help and assistance you require than your neighbors. In the vicinity where you hope to get a property, ask questions from people who are better experienced than you are. Walk up to your neighbors politely and ask questions about their experience with tenants. They will have good information to give you, and it would prove helpful to you in dealing with the management of your property. A trivial mistake in handling your property and tenants would result in a drastic turn of events for you and may even cost you the benefit of your profit.

You need to be sincere in dealing with your neighbors. Explain your intention to them and state what you hope to get out of the property. When you explain to them that you intend to purchase your property, you also need to ask them how they manage the affairs of their tenants. Do not be limited to asking your neighbors alone. You need to see for yourself. Drive around the neighborhood and see what it looks like. A look at the environment will give you an insight into how the neighborhood thrives on a daily. It would also confirm your opinions on the neighborhood. In surveying the environment, go at different times to see how it looks. There are chances that the neighborhood looks different during the morning, afternoon, and evening.

Additionally, maintain a close rapport with landlords. The landlords in the neighborhood have had a lot of experience as to what managing a property entails. Join a landlord association and become part of the process. Allow them to guide you and give you all the information you need to become a successful landlord. The information from the landlords will save you from starting the wrong way. Being a landlord or property owner is easy when you have the right kind of information that would help you become successful.

In situations where the property you want to purchase has some existing tenants, ensure you ask questions about the tenants and how best to interact with them. For all you know, the tenants may have been a major reason the previous owner of the property wants to sell the property. Do not underestimate the roles of tenants in the choice of property. Whilst tenants can be a great source of financial breakthrough, they can also cause your ruin.

Seek advice from the previous owner of the property and learn from his personal experiences. Contrary to what most people think, asking questions or seeking advice doesn't make you weak. It explains your zeal and interest to get it right. As a first-time investor, it is extremely necessary to do what is appropriate. No one goes wrong with the right kind of information. A lot of mistakes investors make in rental property investing is the inability to get the right kind of advice. There is certainly going to be information you have no idea about, and unless you go out of your way to find out the right state of things, you will end up with loads of mistakes.

Furthermore, you need to learn to do away with your ego. One factor that mitigates your purpose will be ego. The manner in which you approach your neighbors, previous property owner, and landlords will determine how eager they would be to assist you. If you present yourself as one who doesn't care about their opinion and actions, you will never get it right. Irrespective of the way the various individuals in the society behave, there would always be someone who is ready to help you with the necessary information. So, ensure you make your neighbors realize that you mean no harm and are willing to learn from them. There are chances that your neighbor, previous property owner, and even the landlords will keep certain details away from you. They could have a change of heart if you approach them with a friendly attitude. No one likes to associate with an individual who is full of himself.

Every information and advice you require to excel as an investor lies in the hands of the people you come in contact. You are the only one who can stop you from being great. Appreciate their existence and be courteous in your approach. A smile won't hurt you. You can begin with a simple compliment or a polite greeting. Then, try to become friends with them.

Introduce yourself to them politely. Do not assume they know your intention. They wouldn't know unless you state your purpose in the environment. Also, when you want to approach, have a respectable appearance. A lot of people are security- conscious. If you do not look like a responsible fellow, they may not see the need to listen to you.

*****

CHAPTER FOUR

PROFESSIONAL PROPERTY ASSESSMENT

When getting a property, it is necessary to consult a professional who is better equipped and experienced in issues related to property management. Purchasing a property is a huge financial decision for anyone to make. It involves a lot of knowledge, information, and resources. A single mistake can blow away your investment. So, it is always best to do what is essential for your investment. There are certain features to look out for before paying for a property. You may have successfully sourced the finance needed for the property. Nonetheless, it is not a good enough reason to settle for just any property. Before you make the payment for the house, take a deep breath and ask yourself if you have done all that needs to be done. Remember, this is your investment and can generate you a lot of good if you look at all the factors critically.

You may not be able to do this all by yourself. You need someone to assist you- an individual who is better experienced in real estate matters. Get a professional! The professional understands all there is to purchasing a property and can identify red flags from a mile away. Can you? No, you can't!

Assessing the property ensures you adequately tackle every issue that may emerge in the course of owning the property. Any wrong attempt in acquiring a property mars your objective and mocks the effort you have made so far. To avert such unpleasant situations, engage the services of a real estate agent to survey the property critically and inform you if it is a worthy investment. A lot of people assume there is no need to hire the services of a real estate agent because they can do it alone. Listen! Property assessment goes beyond the physical structure of the property. It addresses other areas of the property. You have a poor investment plan if you spend more money on the repairs of the rental property than the actual cost of purchasing the property. All of this can be avoided if you just wait for what is right for you. In circumstances where you fail to have an inspection carried out on the property, you could end up with a liability instead of an asset.

As soon as you discover the property is not a worthy investment, you can make the choice of either forgoing such investment or making something good out of it. The choice you make will be solely governed by your intention of getting the investment in the first place. The original plan is to get an investment that would yield another source of income to you. If it goes outside that plan, then the investment is not worthy. After the inspection on the property has been done, you will know of any hidden defects or extreme malfunctioning on the property. This would help inform your opinion and actions.

The property assessment is not only limited to the physical parts of the property but also the sustainability of such an investment. A property manager knows about these inspections and is in a better place to guide you on the right steps to take. One of the factors the property manager considers in inspecting the property is the environment where the property is located. The environment is very important in purchasing a property. When you make a mistake in the choice of environment, it can affect everything about that property. Hence, you need to find out about the neighboring houses close to the property you want to purchase, as well as the amount of rent that is paid on those properties. What is the future for the property? Will the rent increase or decrease? The answer to these questions will determine what you are expected to do. This would aid you to come to an understanding of the worth of the property in the future and if you would benefit from selling it at a later time.

If you do not feel the rental property is a worthy investment or you do not think you are prepared to handle all the expenses of a repair, you can settle for a property that is rent- ready. Such properties are very affordable and can be easily put up for rent. Investing in a rental property is not too much of a problem provided you have the right information at your disposal. A rent-ready apartment generates income for you almost immediately after you purchase the property. This is because you have little or no repairs to make on the property. It ensures that, as an investor, you are not going to plunge into something that wouldn't be of benefit to you. Rent- ready property is the best option for new investors. Such investors may not have the needed information that is used for making repairs on a property. To play safe, it is advisable for new investors to go for rent ready property because of the numerous advantages attached to it. As a matter of fact, purchasing a rental property is not in any way difficult or complicated; it only seems like a daunting task when the property is a mess. Then, the investor will be saddled with the responsibility of ensuring the property is almost new.

It is paramount for the investor to bear in mind that the assessment of the property is not the sole responsibility of the property manager. The investor also has a role to play by ensuring the property meets his required standard and is the exact property he wishes to acquire in terms of finance and other related topics. It is wrong for the investor to stay in the dark about the activities that revolve around the intended property. There is no better way to be an investor by contributing not only your finances but also time and available resources. Unless you pay attention to the state of your property, the property manager may not do good work in terms of assessing the property.

Additionally, the help of a real estate agent makes it easier for you to pay the actual worth of the house. As a new investor, you may not understand market values and can get cheated into paying extravagant sums for a house. The chance of overpaying for a property is minimized or completely eliminated. After the inspection has been performed, you will get the right information on the worth of the property you hope to purchase. The inspection also looks for the conditions of the property, such as roofing, ceiling, electricity and other issues that may spring up in the course of time. These factors, if not properly addressed, can become a problem for the investor who has purchased the property.

Property assessment also involves verifying all the information you may have been given. It doesn't end at going through the property and finding out about its structures. It also requires that you find out the true state of the situation for yourself. How accurate can the information you have been given be? You may never find out unless you access the property yourself. Earlier in the course of this book, I stated that there is no such thing as being too careful in making an investment. You need to be careful at all times to avoid pathetic stories. If you do not want to be caught up in fraudulent transactions and misleading information, ensure to find out things for yourself. There is no harm trying to find out things for yourself; after all, it is your intended property. Be in the know of the things that affect the property.

It is necessary to look out for factors like asbestos, mold, and radon. These are small factors but are not to be treated lightly. Asbestos is sometimes present on a property. When you intend to buy a rental property, ensure that the property inspector looks out for the presence of asbestos. Asbestos can negatively influence the cost of repairs on a property. This can be adequately avoided when the inspector unveils the presence of this factor. More so, it can affect the cost at which you can resell the house. It is always possible that you will put up the property for sale even after purchasing it. The next investor may not be willing to pay as much as you have on the rental property. So, it is important to stay careful and make the right choice.

When there is mold on an intending property you hope to acquire, the inspector can easily identify it. Mold is easy to correct should you want to buy the property, but failing to identify the presence of mold can adversely affect your respiratory system. You wouldn't want a situation where the property affects the health of your tenants who would pay rent to you. It wouldn't speak well of you as a property owner to have an apartment that affects the health of your tenants. More so, there are many health-related problems associated with mold. It is acceptable to go on with acquiring the property, but you need to understand what acquiring such property entails.

The presence of radon in an apartment affects the water and air. Unlike mold, radon is very difficult to get rid of. No matter how simplified the topic looks, radon is not to be joked with. Any property that has the presence of radon needs to be taken seriously. More so, the cost of fixing a radon- ridden apartment is also very expensive, and this means you will incur a huge cost in trying to fix the problem.

Property assessment is to be done in proportion to your financial strength. You need to understand that the property inspector will also be paid for services rendered. All of this will affect your finances if you do not manage it accordingly. Don't go for a property that is unrealistic. This implies buying a property that is above your budget. Work in accordance with your plan. Don't go outside your scope to get a property.

The choices you make should be in accordance with the amount you have mapped out to acquire a property.

Assessing the property also requires finding out the potential growth of the investment. If the property will not yield good returns, the property inspector will inform you of the risks involved in purchasing such properties. Do not assume that such risks are inconsequential. It is essential to ensure that you understand everything there is to the property to avoid a situation where you would not understand what you have gotten yourself into.

Rent ready apartments may limit your purchase options, but it is a secure way of making an investment. Making an investment is not solely dependent on mere interest but on the stability of the property to generate desired returns. With rent-ready properties, there is an opportunity for your investment to grow into something very big that would generate good returns for you.

In all, property assessment protects your interest as an investor and ensures you are not involved in the wrong kind of deal. The importance of assessing a property before purchasing it is actually unlimited and involves a lot of research, dedication, time, and resources. But an interesting fact is that it is worth it in the end. So, if you hope to make the right decisions in purchasing a property, engage the services of a professional to assist you with the needed guidance and professional support.

*****

CHAPTER FIVE

DOCUMENTATION AND PROPERTY MANAGEMENT

Professionalism is the bedrock for every business to thrive. The success or failure of any business relies a great deal on the modus operandi of such a venture. In managing a rental property, a property owner is faced with two options: managing the property himself or engaging the services of a property manager. Whatever options the property owner favors, it is important to spell out the duties and responsibilities of all the parties involved in the transaction.

It is essential to have formal documentation of your investment information. This should not be taken for granted. The documentation of your investment is legal and assures you do not experience any disagreement or conflicting issues about your property in the near future. Most times, a first - time investor does not entirely understand what it entails to own a property, and this can amount to a lot of mistakes in the course of handling the property. To prevent such problems, it is important to employ the services of a seasoned property manager who would guide you into making the right choice.

There is absolutely nothing wrong in handling the property yourself. As a matter of fact, it is the easiest way to learn what being a property owner involves. More so, there is no better way of learning about situations other than experiencing them first-hand. But, in doing this, ensure you have the appropriate documents in place. The reason for this is paramount. Handling your property entails you come in contact with a whole lot of issues, which would entail supervising the property and coming in contact with your tenants. Not all tenants are stubborn or difficult to manage, but it is best to play it safe. As the landlord of your property, there should be a formal agreement between your tenants and you. The agreement must specify the conditions attached to living on your property. This is essential so that, when a tenant is found wanting or acting against the signed documents, you can take the necessary actions needed to protect your property.

The documents necessary for property management are:

Lease agreement: The lease is considered to be the most important document that a property owner must possess. This agreement is legally binding the tenant to the conditions of living on your property. It also specifies the amount the tenants are expected to pay for rent, when they should pay their rent, and how the property should be managed. If at any point in time a tenant violates this agreement, you are at liberty to seek justice in the arms of the law. As a first-time investor, do not assume you understand all there is to the lease agreement. You may need to consult the counsel of individuals who are experienced in that regard. Feel free to seek advice when need be. The lease agreement also governs your attitude towards the property. So, make sure you also abide by the dictates of the lease. Additionally, whatever means of payment you think is suitable or convenient for you should be stated in the lease agreement. The reason for a lease agreement is to ensure that both parties are not unduly treated. If there is any dispute between you and the tenants, you can quickly reference what is stipulated in the agreement, and the issue could be resolved amicably. The relationship you would foster with your tenants is solely dependent on the manner you draw your lease. Most importantly, spell out the laws that would govern your property. It is always necessary to get it right from the word go.

Rental application form: There is also a need for the rental application form. Remember, real estate is not child's play. There is no such thing as being too careful. If protecting your interest as an investor means you are overly careful, indulge in it! This document consists of the renter's information and covers very important details, such as the renter's credit card information. Immediately after you put up your house for rent, there would be a lot of renters who indicate their interest on your property. This document contains all the information about different renters and helps you to make the right decisions in selecting a suitable tenant for your property. When considering a tenant to stay on your property, the tenant would be expected to submit photocopies of their identity cards, as well as proof of their income. Now, this would aid you to select the right tenant who is fit to rent your house. Nonetheless, do not forget to run a background check on the prospective tenants before you make your final decisions.

Rental laws: You need to know the laws of the state that govern real estate. Knowledge is undeniably power. The right knowledge of real estate will help you to do what is best for your property. Should you go contrary to the laws governing real estate, be ready to face the risk of accumulating loss. A careless mistake from your end as a property owner can cost you the desired profits you intend to make off the property. Your tenants are also at liberty to make use of the court if they feel you are infringing on their rights. Do well to understand the law of renting out your property because, if a tenant seeks refuge before the court of law, the court will definitely be on the side of the tenant. The effect? You would lose huge sums of money that would be beneficial to your investment.

Sign in sheet: In the course of this book, I clearly stated that rental properties do not bring in immediate sums of money. It is profitable, yes, but do not generate an immediate inflow of money. Notwithstanding, it is always appropriate to do what is best for the property. Plan! You need to have a good plan in mind. Remember, you already have a goal, and your activities must be propelled towards actualizing your goals. So, the right thing to do is to contact all the tenants who are interested in your property. When you have their contact details, it is easier to reach them when you want to lease out the property. One thing is certain; there are a lot of competitors in the real estate industry. When you want to lease your house, always bear in mind that there is another investor somewhere who is ready to lease out his property also. If you fail to do the needful by having proper information of your prospective tenants, they would slip through your fingers and get another property. When you show interest in your prospective tenant, you would always keep in touch with them. By so doing, you are also protecting your interest and that of your property. Another advantage of doing this is that, when you have their information, it is easier for you to select the best from the pool. A lot of people will indicate interest, but you can't have everyone on your property. So, with the aid of a sign-in sheet, you can select the ideal tenant for your property.

Rent calculator: As a property owner handling the investment, you may not have the time to pay attention to the way the rent is paid. No one wants to incur too many losses and few profits. So, the best way to go about this is to make use of the rent calculator. This calculator helps to keep accurate information on the way the rent is paid by tenants. Therefore, you can be far away and yet so close. Never underestimate the task involved in handling properties. It is not as easy as it seems. If you fail to account for the rent your tenants pay to you, then you are doing a poor job as a property owner. Another added advantage is that rent calculators also reveal the move in and move out time of the tenants on your property. Last, it minimizes the conflict that is most likely to arise on the issue of rent.

Move-in and move out form: One thing is sure about rental properties. No tenant is willing to stay too long on a property. Different structures are bound to be erected every day. These tenants are always going to find reasons to leave your property. It could be on relocation grounds, change of job, or something as little as a mere choice. Whatever be the case, your tenants are going to leave someday. A lot of disputes stem from the issue of move in and move out. You may not have the accurate information required. Your tenant may know but wants to play smart as well. To avoid such ugly situations where you have to banter words with your tenants over the state of your property, it should be documented. This document ensures the property is closely attended to and the chances of a problem adequately avoided. Now, with this form, you will spell out the state of your property when the tenant moved in. This would enable you to carry out a proper analysis for the property when such tenants decide to leave your property. In this regard, you are required to perform an inspection on your property the day the tenant decides to move in. After inspecting your property, you will also document the state of your property, and when they want to move out, you would conduct the same inspection. Both the tenant and the property owner will be actively involved in this process to avoid any doubt on the part of the parties involved.

Notices: This must also be duly specified and documented. There are undeniably very difficult tenants to handle. When you feel you can no longer condone the excesses of a particular tenant, you can give such tenant a notice. This notice should be given a particular timeframe so as to avoid the chances of legal charges. You may not want to go through the rigors of evicting your tenant, but sentiments are not allowed in handling a business venture. If you do not understand how this works, it is best to consult the legal advice of an attorney. Eviction laws are very cumbersome and should be treated carefully to avoid the chances of later regrets.

Furthermore, in cases where you aren't be able to manage the property and want to engage the services of a property manager, you still need to take precautions. The investment is solely yours, and you must ensure that you do not entrust the property to a third party without having proper documentation and an agreement that would describe the terms of the agreement.

The agreement between the property owner and the property manager must clearly spell out the responsibilities of the property owner and the manager, the duration of the contract, the clauses of termination, the type of service to be provided, as well as the fees involved. It is also extremely important that the property owner and manager review the agreement form and make adequate corrections before signing it.

It is also notable to point out that there are numerous advantages attached to engaging the services of a property manager. One reason includes that the property manager is equipped with the necessary information that ensures your property is protected from unlawful activities, professional advice, and diligence in handling the property and saves you a whole lot of stress.

As a property owner, it is your sole responsibility to manage your property manager. It operates more like the checks and balances system of power. You need to be the watchdog over the activities of your property manager. The responsibilities of the property manager include but are not limited to collecting rent, evicting tenants, fostering communications between you and your tenants, handling the move in and move out forms, make repairs, leasing the apartment, screening the prospective tenant application, and offering advice on rent-related issues.

In situations where you engage the services of a property manager, as a property owner, you will not have the liberty of contacting your tenants directly again. If you need to contact your tenants, you need to go through your property manager. Even if you nurture the plans of visiting your property, you still need to consult the services of your property manager. This doesn't nullify the fact that you own your property. It only reveals that your property manager is the intermediary who can access your property and tenants at any given time. Now, you understand why it is extremely important to act as a watchdog on the actions of your property manager. If you fail to follow up with the actions of your property manager and have proper legal documentation between both of you, you may end up losing your property to the wrong hands.

As a rental property owner, your responsibilities include but are not limited to paying insurance, tax, utility bills, and compensation fees. It is clearly evident that inasmuch as a property manager handles the affairs of the property directly, you never stop playing a major role on your property. So, one way or the other, you are also a property manager but in an indirect manner.

Documentation and property management is a core aspect of investing in real estate property. The documents show that your business is legally recognized and ensures that every other individual who makes contact with your property will attach some level of importance to it. All the necessary documents must be in place, whether you intend to handle the property yourself or get another person to do your job. More so, in engaging the services of a property manager, never be in a hurry to trust your partner completely. For every business venture to succeed, there should be a deep level of commitment to it. It is your responsibility to man the affairs of your property irrespective of the presence of a property manager. However, working with a property manager who is sincere and transparent in his dealings brings forth a desirable level of success in the business venture.

*****

CHAPTER SIX

CONSIDERING ECONOMIC AND RENTAL VALUE

Rental properties are a good investment, but it is also important you get the right understanding of the values of the property. There are two major determinant factors in rental property investment. They are the economic and rental value of the property.

The economic value of a property fluctuates for various reasons. There are no certainties in the economic situation of countries. Different factors contribute to an economic downturn. It is necessary for investors to make the right decision when investing in rental properties. Getting an environment that is profitable, irrespective of the various economic cycles of the country, is a wise factor for every investor to consider.

There are risks in rental property investment. But, this risk can be controlled with the right steps. Only seasoned investors understand the importance of assessing a property thoroughly before purchasing it. A new investor may not understand what investing in rental properties entails. Thus, it becomes a problem for the new investor. For this reason, first-time investors are always encouraged to make the right decisions in regard to investing in rental properties. As a matter of fact, purchasing a property in an environment that is relatively known to encourage a lot of rental homes will not be affected by fluctuations in the economy. Despite the economic fluctuations and downsize of the population, there are a large number of individuals who still crave a place to stay and will be willing to pay the rent for a suitable place. A suitable environment or location will minimize the risk associated with investing when there is an economic meltdown.

Before making a decision to invest in rental properties, it is important to consider the different economic cycles and how they can affect your investment. It is generally believed that the most appropriate time to make an investment is during the recession cycle. As an investor who desires to delve into rental properties, it is important you make good use of the recession cycle to make your investment. The benefit of investing during the recession cycle is the advantage of getting a good rental property for an affordable price. Though, there are also some risks associated with making an investment during the recession stage because there are a lot of uncertainties about the recession period. The recession period is generally classified as a period when there is a rise in unemployment, inflation, and the inability for individuals to pay for rent. Inasmuch as this can be a profitable business to venture into at that particular period, the benefits are also too good to be overlooked. Purchasing a property during the recession period makes it easier for you to sell the property when the economic cycle moves from the recession period to the recovery stage. During the recovery stage, the economy is no longer plagued with the uncertainties of unemployment and other issues that affect economic growth. At the recovery phase, there is a positive improvement in renting properties, and as such, investors make good profits. The peak phase is regarded as the best economic cycle. It is the period when investors get the proceeds from their investment.

More so, the peak phase is characterized by the birth of new ideas that are centered on economic growth and development. It also involves the availability of jobs for individuals in the country. All of these factors are very important for an investor to recognize.

It is also important to emphasize that inasmuch as all properties are adversely affected by the recession of a country, some countries actually do better than others. Unless an investor has the right idea about the various types of rental properties he can invest in, he will not be able to make the right choice. A typical example of rental property investing that survives the recession period more than the other types is the multifamily rental property. Investing in multifamily property assures the investor a good source of passive income because of its structure. Analytically, no matter how difficult it is in a country or how hard the recession hits, a typical family will still consider the importance of shelter to every other factor. This shows how important the multifamily rental property is. This type of property is always in high demand, despite the situation of the economy. Additionally, a majority of them are positioned in a good location.

> ### The impact of the economy on the different rental properties value

Holiday / Vacation homes: This type of rental property is mostly affected during a recession period. The benefits of investing in a holiday/ vacation rental home are tremendous, but such an investment is also prone to become a liability during the economic crisis. The reason is not far- fetched. A lot of individuals would rather put their money to good use, such as purchasing groceries or paying up their mortgage, rather than indulge in a vacation trip. This adversely affects the investor who would experience difficulty in getting guests who are going to pay the rent on the vacation home. In fewer cases, where guests are willing to pay the rent for a vacation home, the rental value of the property decreases, and this affects the income of the investor. For investors who are looking to invest in vacation/ holiday homes, they need to be aware of the risk attached to such investment. To avoid an unfavorable situation for the investor, it is strongly advised that the investor makes his investment in an environment with a low supply of vacation homes. In this situation, the investment of the investor is protected because there will be minimal competition. By doing this, it would help protect the economic and rental value of the property at all times.

The choice of location for a holiday/vacation home protects the property from depreciating in value. The quality of real estate investment is that it appreciates over a period of time, but in cases where the investment becomes more of a liability than an asset, it is likely to depreciate. Moreover, the vacation home can also make up for your second home of residence in the nearest future. Hence, it is important to make decisions that will positively affect the property. The use of a marketing firm, like AirHub, helps to ensure that, as an investor, you still make money off your property. It helps to attract guests to your vacation home that are capable of paying for short rentals.

Multifamily rental properties: Multifamily rental properties are usually a common form of rental properties investors settle for. The reason is not far-fetched. There are lots of benefits attached to investing in multifamily rental property. One of the foremost benefits is the ability to generate income from the business venture. However, location is a major criterion to look for when investing in multifamily properties. The location of the multifamily rental property determines if it becomes a profitable business venture. The benefit of the multifamily rental property makes it the most favored amongst other types. For this reason, investors delve into it at all times. Like it was stated earlier, multifamily rental properties survive recession well compared to the different investment types. This is unarguably true. But, in making an investment, it is necessary to consider the different economic cycles that are prevalent in any country. A good instance is a post-recession phase. What happens to the multifamily investment? During the post-recession phase, the multifamily investment suffers the most. During the post-recession period, the effects of the recession are greatly reduced, and this makes it possible for individuals to live better. This prompts a lot of individuals to make an investment in multifamily property. The effect of this is that a lot of multifamily properties become concentrated in a particular location, especially an environment characterized by affordable rental properties. This makes it difficult for you to get good returns on your property as a result of the increase in competition.

Nonetheless, investing in multifamily properties is the safest rental property to invest in, as its economic and rental value is not thoroughly affected during the different economic cycle.

Factors that help a rental property stand out amidst economic downturn

Location: Location is of utmost importance in getting a rental property. The location of a rental property makes it desirable even amidst the economic situation in a country. The truth is that a lot of people still have money to throw around, even in the face of recession. Such individuals are willing to pay the rent on a property that meets their needs. This is a major reason potential investors are encouraged to seek the guidance of a property manager before making decisions about getting a property. When a property is located in a strategic position with a lot of attractive features around it, a large number of people will indicate interest in such a property irrespective of its cost. Though, when the economic bites hard, the rent on a property is affected. But, it wouldn't be so hard if the property meets the renter's specification.

Furthermore, properties that are within a walkable distance from the renter's workplace will be the first choice of a renter despite the cost of the rent. Suffice to say, the location of a property plays an important role in determining if its economic value or rent value depreciates with prevailing economic situations. As such, the decisions that are made about the location of a property determines if it is recession-proof.

Size of the land: The size of the land where the property is situated is also an important factor to be thoroughly examined in getting a property. The returns on the investment can also be measured by the available space on the land. Land space can be used for other benefits besides the property that is situated on it. Renters will quickly settle for a property that has sufficient space that may be used for various activities, such as gardening, car space, and a whole lot of other features.

Additionally, in considering the economic and rental value of a property, it is important to bear in mind the need to secure a property in an environment with lots of apartment buildings. In a place where there are lots of apartment buildings, renters are easily attracted to such a place. The math of rental property investment is to think like the renter. For instance, what would attract you to a property? The typical answer to that is an environment that is characterized by a lot of apartment buildings that are different from what you are used to, right? Exactly! That is the same thing that a potential renter will look forward to. By investing in such a place, you do not have to spend much on advertising. The advertising cost on your rental property will be thoroughly reduced, making it possible for you to generate money from the investment while making profits at the same time.

> **How to measure the value of a rental property**

When investing in rental properties, you need to accept the reality that you must access your property so as to determine if you are making profits.

The sales approach: In measuring the value of your property, sales is a common determinant factor. You need to make a comparison of the amount your renters pay for rent and the amount that is paid on other properties. To achieve this, you need to examine the amount that has been spent on renting out other properties over a period of time. Measure how rent fluctuates at different periods. The way the rent of a property fluctuates will provide insight into what it would be in years to come. Furthermore, the rental value of a property is also determined by certain features of the properties, such as the type of apartment it is, the number of rooms in the apartment, as well as the design of the apartment. As long as the property stands out from other properties in that vicinity, the tendencies for such apartment to be rented at a high price is relatively high. Your taste and choice of a property may be entirely different from that of the renter. This is why it is important to think like the renter before making a decision on the kind of property you want to purchase. Thus, ensure you carry out a comparative analysis of the market type and size before making your final decision in purchasing a property.

Capital pricing model: This method is effective in measuring the net income expected from the property. In this method, the investor is aware of the cost of purchasing the property. The cost of purchasing the property includes the cost of maintenance and operations. It further analyzes the place of risk when making an investment. More so, it gives insight into the different available opportunities for the investor to choose from. Thus, it analyses the investor's return on investment from the rental property he hopes to invest in. As such, the investor makes decisions based on the rental property and compares the risk involved in the investment to other investment types. In situations where the risk of making the investment outweighs the return on investment of the rental income, there is really no need to proceed with such investment. Such investment doesn't add positive financial impact on the part of the investor. To avoid an unpleasant financial situation, the investor avoids such investment. A typical example is when an investor purchases a property that is already looking old and needs repairs. Such an investor will definitely incur more costs on paying for the repairs on the property, and this would affect his rental income. Likewise, purchasing a property in a high crime environment, the investor will certainly pay a lot of money on security. This suggests the investor must properly weigh the risk associated with making an investment and how it affects the profit from the business.

The income formula: This is a method every investor must favor. This measures the income from the property compared to what was paid to purchase the investment. Every investor goes into business with the view of making money. This method is used for measuring rental income from investment. This is mainly used for measuring commercial properties.

Gross rent multiplier approach: This method is used to measure the investor's profit in a year. The profit of the investor is measured by the rent he gets from the renters on his property every year. This method is necessary to help the investor make decisions about his investment. It is the easiest way for the investor to determine the worth of the property. However, it doesn't involve the cost of the other expenses on the property. There are bound to be other expenses the property will incur. This has to be calculated before the investor calculates the exact worth of the property. The other expenses that are incurred on the property involve the cost of utilities, taxes, and maintenance. Although this is quite similar to the income method, the gross rent multiplier approach makes use of this method to calculate the rental value of a property.

The cost method: This is used to measure the exact worth of a property and the income it can generate. To achieve the cost of a property and its value, the investor calculates the land value of the investment, as well as the cost of the repairs on the property. This method is best used when determining the rental value of a property when it is new rather than for older properties. When you want to ascertain the proper value of any special property, this method is the best method to apply.

In all, there are no best way to measure the value of a property. There are various methods of measuring the value of the property. Any investor who wants to delve into rental property investment needs to evaluate the property critically from all sides. An insight into these various methods will help the investor make the right choice. When you find a rental property you want to invest in, ensure you weigh the economic and rental value of the property to ascertain if it is a good investment.

*****

CHAPTER SEVEN

MARKETING AND ADVERTISING

If you're purchasing a new property or renovating the old and you're out to get new tenants, you need to go through marketing and advertising class all over again. Marketing does not happen without conscious effort. It's not magic but a whole lot of work.

Before you go about advertising your property, you need to have an idea of your target market. You need to study their demographics, as well as their psychographics. Be acquainted with their behaviors, beliefs, and their interest. Make use of apps like survey monkey for your primary research.

To aid in your marketing plan, ask yourself these questions:

- Where would people go when in need of an apartment?
- What basic amenities are the deal breakers?

- What sort of community would renters prefer?

To answer all of the above, you need a STRATEGY. So, create one.

Below are strategies to fuel your marketing and advertising plans.

1. As earlier emphasized, know your target market. When you're able to narrow them down, finding them would be easy. Apart from that, be current in the day to day activities of your neighborhood. Know who is moving in and who is moving out and show concern to the community needs. You need to let them know you're not just a landlord but good townsmen too.

2. In this 21st century, everyone has two or more social media accounts, not to mention a business-oriented person like you. Social media is a powerful tool in the hands of business owners these days, so doesn't underestimate its power and importance. You

don't have a social media account for your property? Create one now. Instagram and Facebook or Pinterest are your best shot, as they offer uploads of pictures and content. This would enable you to take pictures of your property and entice your prospective audience. Never go a day without posting. Consistency is important. Let your online presence be top-notch.

3. Talk to people. As powerful as social media is, you cannot rule out the traditional method of advertising. Referrals are magical. You cannot stop people from talking, so why should you stop talking? Use this as a weapon to advertise your property. Tell someone to tell another that there's a property up for rent somewhere. Don't forget to ask your customers to drop their comments on your website and go further by giving them gifts if they refer someone to you. No one refuses freebies. Give a little

appreciative gift for every new person they bring and watch the magic happen.
4. Be interested. You've got all the renters you need. Are you going to stop there or think of your tomorrow? You can engage yourself in helping others rent their properties as well. Get a list of interested renters and make it a sign of duty to keep them updated about another rental opportunity; by so doing, you would always be in business and never run out of prospective client/renters.
5. Strive to be like a flowing river that constantly gives to smaller ones. Be on good terms with the community that harbors your property; be connected. Imagine you've got 2 or more properties in a community. You would be well-known, but your popularity would not be valued if you've not made any positive impact in their lives. Do something remarkable for the community church or school, be involved in town meetings or festivals, organize programs,

or have a charity fare. When you are positively connected to the community, they would be your leading marketing team. Automatically, you become a trusted figure, and you would always come highly recommended.

6. Again, be mindful of the community, not just your building. As much as you want to advertise/ market your property, don't forget it dwells in a community. Remember one way to know your target market is through their demographics, which means before your property became known to them, the community would have appealed to them first. There is no family without a community and vice versa.

So, if the community has great amenities and wonderful views, sell it alongside your building. Let the renters know about the shopping mall or the recreation center, the community library, or senior homes and loads more. Market all these as well. Renters would probably place more value to your property.

Marketing and advertising your rental property is not entirely limited to the above-named factors that have been listed. You need to be cognizant of time. In every business venture, time is of the essence. A lot of factors are directly related to time, and this includes how you to advertise your rental property. A lot of property owners or first-time investors do not make adequate use of time in advertising their properties. There is a great benefit in being time conscious of all marketing related activities of your property. In marketing your property, there is absolutely no need to wait for your current tenant to vacate the apartment before getting someone suitable.

As a property owner, you need not wait for a tenant to vacate the apartment before making it available for rent. Immediately after the tenant has informed you of his intention to leave your property, you need to make the vacancy public. This is important to prevent any circumstance that would make the house vacant after the existing tenant leaves.

One important fact to bear in mind is that getting a suitable tenant takes a couple of months. So, to save time and to prevent unnecessary wasting of time, it is necessary to begin the search for a new tenant in an appropriate time. In cases where the potential tenant is interested in seeing the apartment for rent, inform the existing tenant duly so as to avoid any problem from both ends. It is of utmost importance that the factor of time should not be taken for granted. In any activity you get involved in, time is a very important element. Nonetheless, it is also a wise thing to confirm how the law operates in the locality where your property is situated. In some environments, there are certain timeframes in which a property owner can put up his house for rent, especially when there is an existing tenant.

More so, you need to have the proper understanding of who would be attracted to your property. Before putting up your property for rent, you already have a specific type of tenant you hope to occupy your property. Do not accommodate any tenant if they do not meet with your specification. Get familiar with the Federal Government laws of the country where the property is and avoid any form of discrimination on protected citizens. Be conversant with the population in the environment and what is important to them. The environment the property is situated in will most likely attract individuals who prefer living in such an environment. In a situation where the property is situated close to a student environment, the chances are that the property will attract more students than family-based individuals. The reason is not far-fetched. The demand for property will be very high among the students. So, to facilitate the advertising process, go to the college and find out what it takes to advertise in the school environment. The advertisement fee in the school environment will be cheaper, and the chances are that it would reach a large number of people. Though, quite a number of schools provide off-campus accommodation for students who want to live away from the school environment. Nonetheless, give it a try and do not be discouraged.

You can also make use of a sign. The internet has played a major role in advertising products and services. Nonetheless, one major thing to consider is that, before the advent of internet and tech ology, people found a way of advertising their products and services through the use of signs. It may sound very unbelievable, but a lot of people still pay attention to signs and take it quite seriously. Putting up a sign that indicates the availability of a property for rent is a great means of advertising your rental property. A lot of people will indicate interest or may even refer someone to your property. If you want your sign to stand out and attract the right kind of people, it is essential to look out for basic features that your property must possess. To get a good sign that would do the needed magic, make sure it gets a professional look. You wouldn't want a situation where your prospective tenants may be discouraged by the physical look of the sign. Most individuals wouldn't want to consider an apartment or property that is not properly written. Put up a sign that is very attractive and professional. Make sure the sign is informative and set to accommodate everyone. Additionally, put the sign in a strategic position where the sign would be easily visible to everyone even from a far distance. Give it an eye-catching touch. Put up attractive symbols alongside the sign that would make people pay attention to it. Also, consider the use of attractive colors in building the rental sign. Then, ensure that the location on the sign is accurate. You also need to ensure the sign is visible for everyone that comes across it. The sign also needs to include your personal contact information to make it easier for interested persons to contact you about the property for rent. You can also choose to include information about the property, such as the type of apartment it is as well as the number of bedrooms on the property. To spice up the details of the rental property, you can choose to include juicy details of the apartment, such as the amenities that are within close range to the property.

There are also various online websites that you can use for advertising your property. These online websites constitute a major part of the advertising process. There are a variety of websites that serve to connect prospective tenants with different property owners. The various online sites are used for different postings and to get the right kind of tenants. More so, it will help you to market your property to suitable tenants. The number of property owners that makes use of online websites to reach their tenants is relatively few. But, individuals that have adopted the internet as an avenue for reaching tenants have achieved tremendous benefits attached to using the internet for marketing and advertising rental properties. One gimmick of using Facebook and other social media to advertise your rental property is that you can ask friends to help share your post on their timeline. In this case, you are making it possible for the rental property to reach a lot of people. The advantage of this is that a lot of people will communicate about your property, and this will amount to getting tenants faster than you anticipated.

Make use of pictures. Pictures speak volumes. A lot of people pay attention to images rather than spoken words. The difference between the two is that pictures are basically about showing, while words are based on telling. Ironically, people are easily attracted by what they can see more than what they are told. So, by showing images of the rental property that is up for rent, the chances are that a lot of people will indicate interest in the property. A majority of the time, before people read what you have written, they admire the pictures. Any property that has the right kind of appeal to the senses would definitely stand out from the crowd. If the pictures are properly done, the percentage they would attract a lot of people is greater. However, this can also cost a fortune. Paying for professional photography is really affordable, and as a first-time investor, there are a couple of things that require financial attention. So, you can choose not to contact a professional photographer and just be your own photographer. How? Technology has made a lot of things easier for you. Make use of technology. Your mobile phone can also deliver the same service as professional photography. There are also tons of editing applications that can also provide the same features, like a professional camera. So, make use of all of it to get the exact picture of your property you desire.

Before you commence with it, make sure your property is in proper condition. Take the picture when the property is clean. In that way, you will be able to come up with an appropriate image that will convey the right emotions and expression to your prospective tenants. The only factor you need to be conscious of when taking the picture is the lighting condition of the room. To get the best kind of shot, take the pictures from different angles of the property. You need to show the prospective tenant what your property looks like from different views. In doing so, do not give them a false impression about the apartment. This is one major disadvantage of using images. You can be different by putting up the appropriate images of the property. Then when the tenant comes to inspect the property, he will not be disappointed. Instead, it will instill a level of trust upon the property owner. The only thing that makes you stand out from your competitors is how you package and present your property.

Another interesting way of advertising and marketing your property is to let the prospective tenant have a look at your property. They need to see what they want to pay for. Ensure you also show them around and take them to the strongest point of the property. You can choose to show your property to tenants on an appointment basis. That is whenever they indicate interest in seeing the property. When you give individuals the opportunity to see the property, you are creating a form of awareness and arousing their interest in the property. The right way of arousing the interest of individuals in your property is by creating some sort of awareness of the property. You can decide to rent your property to be used to host an event or function. When you do this, you avail a lot of people the opportunity to see first-hand what your property looks like. Even if they may not have the need for a property, they can choose to refer interested persons to your property, and this would bring about the desired result; you would have a lot of people indicate interest in your property.

Some other tips that would definitely be of help are:

Build yourself as a trusted brand. Add LinkedIn to your social media accounts to portray your professionalism. You are likely to get more professional on LinkedIn; upgrade your skills and build a clientele as well.

You should also think about investing in your property by getting more clients. Run ads when necessary. Look for good platforms that can help you do this. Facebook has the best ad packages for adverts. Leverage on it, even though IG proves good as well.

We all love pictures with content explaining them, but it seems a short video showcasing your property and its wonderful features would give a wow feeling. You can share a short story or have a customer hype you by giving a good recommendation via video. What about you just spice things up and thrill your audience about rentals and what they don't know then watch the number of people that would respond. No long talks, a minute video should do.

Another effective tool for marketing is branding your property manager. They should be your brand ambassador. Equip them with the right tools, appreciate them, and celebrate them and be celebrated in return.

Marketing and advertising your rental property is extremely important in rental property investing. As a matter of fact, it is as important as purchasing the property. Any potential investor who does not pay adequate attention to the importance of marketing will end up having a non-profitable investment. Rental property investing is not a monopolistic business venture. As a matter of fact, there are lots of competitors on the market, and the only way for you to stand out is by making use of the right marketing strategy. Sadly, a lot of potential investors or first-time investors do not understand the place of advertising and go about it nonchalantly.

Marketing your rental property could take some time because you do not want to settle for the least. There are certainly a lot of people who are going to indicate interest on the property, but because you are cognizant of certain factors, you will not be in a hurry to give it out to just any kind of person. This could mean the property will take a longer time to be rented out. Not to worry, you are doing the right thing. Remember, slow and steady wins the race!

As long as you have a very good marketing strategy in place, you have nothing to lose. Allow the process to take its natural course and be grateful that you did. The most important thing in marketing and advertising your property is to get a commendable end result. It mustn't be all about the process but the result. Don't be limited to only one marketing strategy. You can try as many as possible, as long as it is aimed at bringing the right kind of tenants your way.

*****

CHAPTER EIGHT

KNOW YOUR TARGET RENTER

Who is my target renter?

Your target renter can be virtually anybody. It depends on your choice and preference. It could be students, families, or single individuals.

One of the key navigations in rentals is to know your main customers. Remember this business is like any other business out there; the customer is key. Your property definitely can't be for everybody out there. Everyone can't be your tenant, hence the need to know your target market.

Be mindful that, when you decide to target a particular group of persons, it does not mean you try to lay off some or claim they do not meet your standard; instead it's a way of focusing on your target audience, which allows you to concentrate on those who are the real missing piece in your puzzle. This is an efficient way to get to your target market faster.

Let's take a flower shop for an example. The main aim of the flower shops is to beautify the environment. Now, if the flower shop decides to use bank workers as their target market, it would be lucrative, but the purpose of the flower shop would not be achieved. But, if the flower shop decides to try a different target market, such as schools and churches, it would be lucrative. For the real estate industry, if your property is around the college in the community and you're stressing yourself out trying to get married couples to rent, that's way off! Your target market is right there at your fingertips, college students.

With all the illustrations provided, you now have a vivid idea of who your target renter is because knowing your target market means knowing the specific type of individual you want occupying your property.

How do I get to my target renter?

- What do you have at hand? The first thing is to consider your present customer base; if you don't have one, scout the area. If your customer base boldly spells family, you have no business running after college kids. But if you're perhaps scouting, then you can create one based on your findings. You have more students in the area; make your rentals more student-friendly.

- Check out those in the same business. Never overlook competitors. Always keep a tab on them. You need to know what they are doing that you're not or what they are doing that you can improve on. Not asking you to be a copycat, but you don't want to be caught off guard or lagging. Whatever they are doing that's working is worth trying and getting better at it. You need to know what your edge over them would be. Why should the renter choose your property?

- Analyze. You want to appeal to your target market? Analyze your property. What benefits should they be expecting? What is your selling point as a property owner? If you can't put this in place, getting your renters might not be easy.
- Demographics and psychographics. The importance of these two is as essential as they sound. To get your target renter, try to understand some things about them, their age, occupation, income level and so on, very important. Alongside their personality, values and attitudes are key. You can give out questionnaires to get all this.
- Their culture and lifestyle also would be a determinant to many things.

Remember, renters also carry out research on properties and their owners. They are most concerned about the rent price, location, amenities, and so on, and you want to be the first person they come to. Don't forget that you can't accommodate everybody, so you should have eyes for renters who need what you have to offer. The best renter for you is that one person without stress. No need trying to make him see reasons he should reside because all he wants is available.

Know your renter

Don't be too busy or carried away with excitement about your new renter that you forget to run a background check on them. Their demographics and psychographic details are very important. Be sure of why your property was picked. A Google form is a great tool you can use in collecting data. Send them questionnaires, let them fill it out, and you have enough details at your fingertips.

In knowing them, you find out who you're up against. Competitors are everywhere. Studies have shown that one of the reasons people move from one apartment to another or state to state is their constant change of jobs. If your competitors go ahead of you providing what prospective tenants need, you might be at a loss. Always know what your competitors are up to; you either upgrade alongside or beat them to it.

A new family just moved to town, and one of your competitors got the hint before you did and decided to reduce rent for their sake, a loss to you. This implies a need to stay informed at all times. Current industry report or reports from the housing council and the like would help you stay up to date. All these are to enable you to know the demographic change if any arises.

Your renter's needs

Every renter is different, but as a property owner, you need to find the balance. While some are concerned about the air conditioning in the apartment, some are after the ceiling fan; all the same, there are specific things that cannot be ruled out. Some things are paramount and applicable to any new renters.

1. Is the neighborhood safe? Everyone definitely wants maximum security and protection. They want to know if the environment has a low

crime rate and necessary security. You, as the landlord, should have this aspect inspected and give your tenant peace of mind.

2. What's the kitchen like? A prospective renter would want to see a well-equipped kitchen with reasonable space and one with a dishwater, a gas stove, and good water supply. This would be one of their top checks, so you need to see to it to meet their standards

3. I can't do without a bathtub in my bathroom, or a shower is key in my bathroom. Tenants can be choosy, but make sure your bathroom is attractive enough to keep them.

4. What about a game room in your apartment? If space is available, it is a welcomed innovation. Depending on who your target market is, a game room cannot fail.

5. Is your property fenced? If you're looking at accommodating families, you might need to invest in a simple fence around your property. To some tenants, it's a must-have.

6. Gardens are wonderful ideas. Look into it.
7. Outdoor space for relaxation is a killer.
8. With a pool strategically placed anywhere around the house, that's a home run for you.
9. If a parking space can be included, it's a win-win all the same.
10. Above all, just like any other business out there, package your property well. Make sure your presentations are not overhyped but value for their money. Do what is needed to meet your renter halfway through their wants.

❖ **Steps to choosing your target renter**

Your choice of a tenant determines how long your property will last. It is also very true that there are no right or wrong means of screening tenants. But, there is nothing wrong with being careful and doing your best. If you crave perfection or near perfection in handling your property, settle for a tenant using the following steps:

Adhere to the dictates of the law: It is necessary to recognize the place of the law in any choice you make. The government of any country is usually keen on how property owners make decisions concerning the type of tenant to accommodate on their property. Ensure you do not discriminate. It is one thing to be careful and another to discriminate. In your choice of tenant, ensure you do not make negative decisions based on race, sex, familial status, or even religious beliefs. Ensure you do not use such decisions as reasons that would define your choice. The government of most countries will be observant and willing to take appropriate actions against any property owner that makes decisions based on such biased reasons.

Select tenants that are financially stable: You wouldn't want a tenant that is not financially stable, right? Choose your tenants based on their financial strengths. This doesn't presuppose that they must be wealthy. No, they only need to have a comfortable source of income. When your tenants are financially capable, there are chances that they would be willing to pay your rent and fees promptly. There are two ways of checking tenant finances. They are:

- **Verify the source of income:**

It is necessary to get tenants whose monthly pay checks supersede the monthly rent. The only way to get such confidential information is to request their payslip or call their employer and ask relevant questions in that regard. You also need to find out their level of commitment in the organization, their behavioral trait to work, as long as how they attend organization meetings.

- **Credit Check:**

You also need to confirm their credit checks. Find out if they pay their bills at the right time and their debt history. You need to make certain their debt doesn't outweigh their income, or it will be a problem for you to manage. Additionally, make your findings of how long they have stayed on other properties. Find out if they have been previously evicted from a property and if there are situations of bankruptcies in their name. All these will help to inform your decision about the choice of tenant.

Check for any criminal background: It is difficult to hide any criminal involvement of any individual. You can find out the criminal record of any individual from the courthouse because the information is made public. The only thing you will need is the name of such individual, as well as the date of birth. These two items are the only information needed to run a background check on any individual. It is also important to bear in mind that there are cases of fraudulent actions by certain individuals. These individuals do not have their original names publicly revealed, and this may pose a challenge to discovering the true status of such individual. To prevent this occurrence, it is important to have a valid identification card of the supposed tenant and then have the answers to the necessary findings.

Find out how long they have lived on a property: This is an important aspect to consider. An unstable tenant will not have any difficulty leaving your property, no matter how comfortable it is. The best way to gather this information is to ask questions of the previous landlords and confirm the attitude of such individual. You may be surprised to find the previous landlord of such individual kicked such a person off his property for worrisome reasons. The following are good examples of questions you need to ask the previous landlord:

- Do they pay their rent at the right time?
- Why did such an individual leave the property? Were they evicted, or did they just move out on their own free will?
- Did such tenant give a minimum of 30 days notice before such move?
- Did they leave their apartment in the appropriate state?
- Did the individual cause any form of damage on the property?

- How did such person interact with the neighbors in the same environment?
- Were they always eager to lay a complaint?

If the renter is a first-time renter, then there are possibilities that they will not have any rental history. For such category of individuals, ask them to present a guarantor who would sign the lease agreement.

Choose a tenant who is stable in all ramifications: Financial stability is not enough qualification to rent a home to an individual. Also, consider how long they live at properties. On the rental application form, look for how long they stay on a property and why they are so eager to move out of the property. Find out if such a renter also finds it easy to switch jobs and can't stay at a job for a long period of time. If the tenant finds it easy to move out of apartments, there are possibilities that they would do the same to your property, and you will be left with another vacancy. More so, if such a person is not working, they would be unable to pay your rent, and this would not be a comfortable position for you. Worse still, you may have to think about evicting such tenant from your property.

Specify the number of persons to a room: You wouldn't want to have a situation where a lot of people will compete for space in a single room. It would not only result in more repairs but will most likely bring about a lot of noise and disturb the serenity of the environment. This doesn't mean you are being judgmental or biased. You are only doing what you know is the right thing to do. This may not be totally acceptable by everyone. That is why it is important to choose your rentals carefully.

Believe in your choice and decision: There is no better way to do what is right than to follow your instinct. It has earlier been stated that there are no rules for screening a tenant. So, the best person to trust is your instinct. The information documented in the paper can be very misleading because there is every possibility that the individual didn't provide accurate information or may have used another person's identification information. So, the best way to get the right answers is to follow your instinct.

The choice of environment is always important. A lot of people pay special attention to the location of a property. As a matter of fact, the environment the property is located on is as important as the property itself. There are always individuals who are willing to pay good rent to purchase a property. When the property is located in an appropriate environment, it increases the worth of the property. In selecting an area to purchase your property, you need to make sure the property is suitable for good renters. Most individuals crave comfort even in the choice of a rental home.

Also, in the choice of an environment for your property, ensure you look for locations that are equipped with security facilities. Any environment that is not secured will not be attractive to a potential renter. Irrespective of the social class, age or family type, everyone desires to live in a criminal-free environment. You need to understand what purchasing a rental property entails. When renting a property, besides the environment, another factor that renters look for is the safety of such an environment. You do not want to be found wanting in this regard. Do what is necessary to safeguard the interest of your property.

Curb appeal is also a good feature of any environment you settle for. The renters would eagerly be willing to rent a property that is decorated with lots of attractions, such as gardens, well- painted homes, and manicured lawn. All these physical features are extremely important factors that prospective tenants look for before making decisions in the kind of home to pay rent for.

There are definitely going to be competitors in the real estate industry. A lot of investors are also going to strive to get worthy tenants on their property. So, this idea should give you an insight into how to go about it. Your property should be tailored to meet the needs of the prospective tenant. In the case, where you hope to attract college kids, the property needs to be tailored to that specification. Hence, it is necessary to specify the kind of tenants that suit the property. The content and quality of your advertising must be specified in this regard. If individuals do not have this understanding, they may end up renting your property and constituting a nuisance for you. A typical instance is a college kid renting an apartment that is meant for a family home. Such student wouldn't be able to appreciate the content of the apartment and will abuse its use.

A family-based rental property needs to have basic amenities around the vicinity. A typical family home has children who could be in high school or college. This family would appreciate an environment that has a good school structure where their children would be able to attend such schools. More so, there should also be a store or shopping mall in such environment in instances where the family wants to do some grocery shopping.

Students and college kids, on the other hand, will appreciate an environment that provides every basic need they desire. This category of people is in dire need of comfort. So, ensure you meet their expectation, or your property will not be rented for a very long time.

Irrespective of the standards of your prospective tenants, you also need to think about yourself and the interest of your property. Undoubtedly, you need your tenants to contribute significantly to your property by paying rent and keeping your property in good condition. Inasmuch as this is true, you also need to prepare ahead for yourself. How? Protect your interest as well. You need to understand the worth of the property and the amount it can generate for you. It is necessary to consider your return on investment in purchasing any property. In situations where you purchase a property that is inexpensive as a result of its condition, what do you intend to achieve by such a transaction? Your return on investment is dependent on the kind of property you purchase and the area where it is purchased. When you purchase your rental property in a place that is considered below standards, the property will become a liability rather than an asset. To get the very best from a property, research on your preferred neighborhood and come to terms with the amount a property is sold and rented out.

The choice you make in selecting a tenant can be disastrous or helpful. It is solely dependent on the type of tenant you accept to live on your property. It is essential to screen your tenants properly. There are no perfect tenants, but there are tenants that you may not have the capacity to manage effectively. Such type of tenants constitutes a nuisance on your property and will always be a major source of the problems and challenges you encounter on your property. This can be effectively managed by vetting the different rental applications. Accept only tenants that meet your desired specification. Don't lower your standards to suit any tenant. It is only when you compromise in your choice that you settle for less. It is important you know your tenants completely. This implies you need to know everything about them and what they do for a living. Endeavor to check for criminal backgrounds and every other minute detail about them. This information may seem unimportant, but it is of extreme importance that you know the important details about the tenants you hope to accept.

Knowing your tenants should be your first responsibility as a property owner. You may not know the impact a bad tenant can have on your property until you accept them to live on it. The easiest way to have a bad return on investment is to get a bad tenant on your property. Such tenants will only make it difficult for you to enjoy the investment you have plunged into. Any investment that brings about more losses than profit is regarded as a bad investment. The easiest way to get involved in a bad investment is to get a bad tenant on your property.

It is also appropriate to have a lease in place. Your tenants need to be aware of the instructions that surround living on your property. Some tenants are very worrisome and would like an opportunity to refer you to the lease agreement between both of you. On your lease, be sure to specify and address issues appropriately. The tenants need to have an understanding of what is applicable to your property and what is not. Also, specify the lease expiration date and the mode of payment for rent.

*****

CHAPTER NINE

HOLIDAY/ VACATION RENTAL INVESTMENT

Are vacation rentals good investments?

There are no good or bad investments. It only depends on your personal view or philosophy. Note that vacation investment is a totally different kind of investment compared to the residential apartments. Bear in mind that, in vacation rentals, there are no certainties. This implies that you could have an impressive rental year or not. It is good to understand that not every vacation home would make a good rental; you need to know what works and what doesn't.

First things first, what do you intend to do with your rental home? Are you in for the long-term or short-term rentals? For short-term vacation rentals, they are quite flexible and attract higher rental income. On the other hand, long-term rentals require more time and energy; you need to maintain and constantly upgrade at intervals. Unlike the short-terms that have regular cash inflow, the income on long-term might not be that constant.

In sum total, both packages are feasible provided you have the right vacation rental professional at your service.

Before you make up your mind to invest in holiday/ vacation rental property, pay attention to these areas:

Be ready for financial involvement: A lot of people delve into holiday/ vacation rental investment with the mind-set that the returns are almost immediate. Well, that is not always true. Rather than make wrong assumptions on the profits from the property, ensure you have the financial capacity to manage the property. There is no guarantee that, when you purchase a property for an outrageous price, you will recover all the money that you have spent in a couple of months. You may get disappointed if this is the reason behind the purchase. However, it is very possible to get the desired returns when the property is managed effectively. If it isn't, it could take a longer time. Nonetheless, you still need to make adequate preparations for other costs attached to maintain the property.

Consider the place of local laws: The laws are extremely important in making decisions that revolve around investing in properties. In situations where you already have a residential apartment and for personal reasons, you intend to delve into holiday rental property, make sure you ask the appropriate questions to know what is obtainable and what is not. In this case, you may have to check with different stakeholders and applicable zoning laws.

Be aware of various costs: There are going to be some costs you may not be aware of. Make it a point to pay attention to the various costs you may incur in purchasing the property. Costs on utilities, maintenance may be expected monthly. You need to be aware of these costs to make your decisions. This is important to prevent any situation where you would be unhappy or regret the choice you have in such investment.

Furthermore, the cost of the property is crucial. It is not advisable for an investor to pay for a property without considering the financial implication of acquiring such property. Inasmuch as it is permissible to source finance from various sources, it is appropriate to perform a cost analysis of the property and be certain that the property makes financial sense. Calculate the vacancy rates in the chosen environment and be sure it is worth the operational costs on a monthly basis.

A vacation/ holiday rental property is a wonderful investment to make but bear in mind that it may also affect your finances. Some of the cost that you may incur on the property includes paying the property tax, rental income tax, rental home property tax, occupancy tax, operational expenses, property insurance, utilities, HOA fees, management fees, and financing fees.

Have a realistic expectation: As a rule, don't count your chickens before they hatch. This seems to be the problem a lot of investors experience. Do not expect to make your first million in the first year. This is not obtainable! Be realistic. It is essential you bear in mind that, when calculating your income from the rental home, you should also make certain to deduct the monthly expenses you would incur on the property. After the deductions, what you have left is probably your profit. In addition, the investment can make a profit on a seasonal basis. The cost of rent individuals will pay will differ on a monthly basis. There are seasons when individuals pay very high and some when the charge becomes low. You need to recognize these factors when making your calculations.

Get a plan in place: You need a plan to manage your property effectively. Remember, he who plans to fail has failed to plan. Despite your interest in planning, ensure you have a plan that would help you when there are issues. Your plan should revolve around managing the guests and their needs. Without the guests, you don't get paid as such; their comfort should be your utmost priority. It is possible you stay miles away from the rental property. But, what happens when the guests in your rental home experience issues with electricity? Who would attend to their needs? These are questions that should be taken very seriously, and you should also make plans to address such areas. Have you thought about the possibility that your guest may experience difficulty in maintaining the use of the rental home facility and connectivity? All of these are paramount in managing a rental home. You may not be able to do this all by yourself. So, you need the assistance of a readily available property manager, to assist you in this regard. The presence of an efficient property manager will enable you to rest assured that everything is taken care of.

A business plan should be in place: It really doesn't end at purchasing a property. You need to understand how to manage the property. There are a lot of things involved in managing the property. How do you want to advertise your property? If you do not have a worthy plan, you may have issues with managing your properties properly. Ensure you consider an effective marketing strategy or platform where you can tell a large number of the population the availability of your service. If you feel you do not have the energy to manage the marketing of your property, hire a property manager who will see to it.

Keep your property safe: Just like it was rightly stated in this chapter, there are different seasons for the rental home investment. During some seasons, the property will be in use and generate good income for you. But, what happens when it is not in use? When the property is not in use, it is the best time to ensure you protect the property at all cost. If you fail to pay attention to this, your property stands the risk of being subjected to all forms of vandal attacks and activities. You need to think about the appropriate security measures to employ to safeguard your property at all times. A property that is not properly managed will become a liability to you in no time. Endeavor to get a worthy plan that will protect the property at all times.

Some benefits of vacation rentals.

Investing in a vacation home signifies you might have opted for short-term rentals. Preferably, investors are advised to use this avenue to gather the needed experience if it's their first real estate investment. The impressive thing about this is, no matter the nature of your job, real estate investment is the most assured way to make cash outside the regular workday. You might not be aware, but investment in the holiday/vacation home is becoming more demanding and popular these days. So far, it seems to be the best way to become a property investor. Let's take a look at some reasons you should consider vacation investments.

1. You can choose to reside therein and be on holiday as well. Let's assume you own a resort on a private beach. You get to stay there while being on holiday as well. That's why investing in short-term property proves best because, when you've had all the fun with your family and friends, you can comfortably rent it out to some guests in no time.
2. You would experience frequent cash flow. It is an established fact that you can't possibly rent out your property for free. When you're not spending time with your family, you can rent your vacation property and make cool income. Additionally, the return on investment on the holiday rental property is very encouraging. Owning a holiday rental property presupposes that you make money from the property every other day of the month. It doesn't affect your everyday job in the circular world. More so, the finance generated from the daily use of the facility by the guest can also be used to sort out

other needs of the organization such as tax. There is also less financial risk associated with it.

3. What about we sell it? Just as land appreciates, the same is applicable when you're in the long-term investment. Real estate property over time would appreciate in value when the time is right. You can sell off your property at an attractive price and keep all the profits. To make more money, you can do a little bit of renovation to the property, a little upgrade here and there, and it can be sold even at a higher rate.

4. Easily maintained. Unlike other rental opportunities, vacation investment is flexible. Therefore, you can have it as a part-time gig. But if you're not up to the task, you can hire a vacation rental management service. This would ease the pressure from you, and everything would run as it should. The flexibility of the holiday rental property is

evident in the fact that you can choose to rent out the property to the guest or simply use it on a vacation with your family. Either way you choose, you don't lose. The belief behind getting a holiday rental property is for the future. A lot of investors may choose to give out the property on a temporary basis, but when they want to retire, they make use of it.

5. You don't need to evict anyone because they are travelers. They come and eventually leave, unlike the traditional renters where evictions are done and rules guiding tenants are in place; this can be frustrating at times. A lot of business travelers prefer to make use of holiday rental properties rather than any other form of rental properties. This, in turn, has given rise to the number of business travelers, as corporate organizations also prefer to rent holiday rental property on a short-term rental for their employees. This is so because the holiday rental property provides comfort for

the travelers and enables them to conduct their business meeting and activity in a quiet environment.

6. You don't need to do any work. With the holiday rental property investment, you can choose not to be actively involved in the property. Yet, you still get paid. This is the most interesting part of the holiday rental property. The property manager you hire will be charged with the responsibilities of getting things done while providing you with the necessary information. Thus, the property managers will give you the right kind of advice for maintenance and marketing.

Before you consider investing and enjoying the above benefits, ask yourself the following questions:

- Can you stay at your new location for long without getting bored or tired?

- Can you do without jumping from one work to the other? There comes a time when you have to spend weeks on vacation and oversee your property. One of the reasons short term renting is best for you.
- Are you considering keeping it forever? If you can't wait for about 15 years and above, then consider renting on short-term as you can sell off at any time.

Things to consider in choosing a vacation/holiday rental property

The most important thing in any real estate investment plan is a location. Make sure you research to know the best places people would love to visit. Another thing is to get a place that has enough room and can accommodate many people. No one wants to visit a boring holiday site. The choice of a vacation home is dependent on many factors. Inasmuch as it is possible to get a location that best suits you, ensure you consider getting your vacation home in an environment with lots of tourist attractions, such as beaches, casinos, and so on.

The various places where you can get a suitable rental property are through the use of various online sites and the use of real estate agents. The online sites would help you make decisions based on what you are looking out for. It provides different options and images of the available rental properties. Additionally, you get to see the most preferred rental property location, what amenities are present, and why tourists prefer such locations. As a matter of fact, the first place to begin your search is on the internet. You can also make use of the maps to get the location of the rental home and if there are still available vacancies. The advantage of looking online is that it provides a variety of price ranges; as such, you can pick and choose what is best for you. More so, after making your choice from the online site, ensure you hire a real estate agent to help you make the necessary findings of the location you have chosen. The expertise of a real estate agent makes it possible for him to find out every detail about the location, and this would help you make the proper decision. As such, the real estate agent will provide insightful information into the best place for you to purchase your properties and give reasons you need to get such location.

Your choice of a location should be such that would give you an appropriate return on investment and is considerably affordable.

When the location is set, check out your property. Don't be the first-timer who didn't check and gets to complain later. It is the smart thing to do. Do a little bit of comparison and analysis; make sure you're not paying more for less.

Consider the weather and its changes. Would your rental be available all year long? Is the location going to be beneficiary during winter and summer? If this is not checked, you might miss a lot of cash income as your guests' preference is very important.

Relate with the people in the surroundings. What are their likes and dislikes? The dos and don'ts, any taboos? You want to make a good impression on the locals if you want to buy a property in their vicinity. Remember, establishing relationships in real estate is key.

Be acquainted with the rules and regulations guiding vacation holiday rentals. Speak to a professional if need be. In real estate, an agent is all you need to navigate, and the same is expected and applicable in the vacation home investment.

In addition to the above, here are five steps to short-term rental investment.

- **Research-** As earlier mentioned, be sure to know the rules and regulations guiding your choice of investment. Be sure there are standing laws in your location so that locals might not end up changing or adding more to suit themselves. Study your competitors. What are their bookings like? How much do they charge? All these should be part of your research. You don't want to forget to calculate your incomes. Your gross profits, utility bills, the lawn or pool care... what is your revenue? Ask yourself if you're going to make money from this. Make sure you put it all into consideration and always pick properties that would make you more money.

- **The sweet spot**- What is your rental's selling point? What's the view like? The mountains or the beach view? Remember to check what your competitors have going on; you don't want to be below standards. Your basic amenities must be mind-blowing; you have to equip your vacation home with things that would make travelers automatically fall in love with it. Consider what your WOW factor would be, and travelers would make you their first choice.
- **Re-touch the home**- Make your vacation home traveler friendly. This would probably be

your big win. Give them that home away from home feeling, enough towels, and pots of flowers where necessary, nice wall paintings, and lovely furniture and so on. Start building a brand that makes travelers want to come back and even refer you. Don't be cheap in your furnishing.

- **Agents** – In short-term rentals, booking agents expect you to respond to bookings in 24 hours or less, which sometimes might not be visible. You need to hire a company to help you handle all your bookings with swift responses. You can check out sites like *use.warehouse.com or vacasa.com*. They can also help you with your pricing so as not to shortchange yourself. Their job is to make sure everything is done right. They can also help with the cleaning and maintenance of your property. You might just be parting ways with about 10% to pay for their services. Maybe when you're well-established with a good body of staff, you can manage all these yourself.

- **Bookkeeping** – You don't want to owe the government, do you? So, you need to be up to date in the payment of all your taxes regarding your property. You don't want to be out of business even before you start, so always make sure you pay your tax. Sites like mylodge.com can do this for you.

Do you understand the property?

Understanding what your property has to offer can attract the right set of people and the type of travelers that come your way. You need to note that, if your property is an apartment, a condo, a mansion, cottage, cabin or any other type, it can help you locate the right travelers. You can fine-tune your vacation home to accommodate businessmen, families, couples on honeymoon, retired travellers, and the like, depending on you. It would be cool for travelers to know you've created a niche for yourself. You can't be hoping to have a family lodge with you when you own a small apartment. This is where understanding your property comes in.

It would not be a bad idea to create a theme for your vacation rental. Your location can help in creating one. A farmhouse can have a family theme; there is a connection. In addition, your amenities must also agree with your theme and go hand in hand with its interpretation. Free internet, outdoor space, a large pool, maybe a front porch and so many attractive sights, all these are to enhance your property value.

Do not forget to get reviews from your guest. Nice reviews go a long way to getting new travelers.

Is it property at Panama City Beach, Florida or Napa, California? Perhaps it's that old cottage or the nice cabin just lying low? Why don't you just rent it out today!

*****

CHAPTER TEN

NATIONAL AND INTERNATIONAL PROPERTY

At some point, you will find reasons to diversify and broaden your horizon in real estate. Every investor desires to grow in all ramifications, especially as it concerns a real estate industry. There should be a burning desire within you to acquire properties in other parts of the country or even in a different community than the locality you are used to.

Investing in foreign countries requires a lot of adequate research to avoid circumstances of making a terrible choice of a business venture. It necessitates being familiar with the desired society customs and all there is to them.

Purchasing properties in other countries is sometimes a good option for investors because they are most likely going to get the property at a cheaper rate. In most cases, the properties are most likely affordable and bring about a good return on investment for the investors. In buying properties in foreign countries, there are also certain risks involved, but with the right information and research, it will turn out profitable. For those willing to purchase properties abroad, there are some basic steps to be taken to prevent any wrong dealings. Such as:

Don't make hasty decisions: Too many investors are desirous of investing in properties in foreign countries without analyzing the different situations. Some other investors would settle for investing in developing countries because they feel there are higher chances of making profits in those developing countries. It is always risky to arrive at a decision based on unfounded speculation and assumption. When investing in property internationally, the only way to get it right is to avoid decisions that can bring you more harm than good. Do not concern yourself with the factors that surround the developing countries and the fact that other investors succeeded in purchasing properties in those countries.

Investing in international properties is not a blind investment that one should venture into without making due research. Always remember that you have a different drive from that of the other investors. Don't be too quick to make biased conclusions that may jeopardize your investment structure. Before you make up your mind to purchase properties in international countries, you need to analyze the situation and circumstances and come to a conclusion if that is what you really want to do.

Understand the modus operandi of the country: You need to have an idea of what investing in such country entails. All countries possess their own laws that govern rental activities. It is most likely going to be different from your local country. So, don't assume it works the same way everywhere. Ask questions where you do not understand. Make your investigation and research accordingly so that you don't violate the laws of the country and end up incurring loss rather than making profits. It is not enough to have an idea of buying a property at a low cost and selling it at an exorbitant price. It doesn't just end up that way. It actually extends to knowing the laws that govern rental rates, taxes, utilities, and other factors that would most likely affect the property. It may entail reading and consulting books. Whatever it takes, ensure you have the right kind of information. The information you generate would determine if you are interested in buying the property.

Be cognizant of the rental regulations of the country. There would be specified legal information on the rent charges of the country of your choice. Armed with this information, you can then prepare yourself for the amount you will charge the tenants on rent. But, none of this will be realistic unless you make a realistic plan on how to achieve your aim.

Don't invest everything you have: This is a very important step to be cognizant of. A lot of investors make this mistake. It is important to emphasize that the fact that a property is cheap doesn't make it the right kind of property to invest in. The property may be cheap but would involve a lot of unnecessary expenses. Undoubtedly, life is a risk, but there are times when you need to be more practical in your approach. Investing in international properties should be done one step at a time. You do not fully understand all there is to the country. Do you know if their laws are stringent or flexible? As a first-time investor, don't be too carried away with the cheap cost of a property and invest all your financial resources into it. It is acceptable to make an investment but do not throw caution into the air. Better still, invest in low- cost properties even if the profit is not so good. It is better to acquire a property at a low cost and make a little profit than acquire a property that wouldn't give you the return value.

Invest in commercial properties: As the name presupposes, commercial properties are bound to generate a good source of revenue. More so, they are a relatively safer choice of an investment property. With commercial properties, you are assured of a secured means of generating rent on a steady basis. Examples of commercial properties include shopping malls and hotels. These properties are good ways of generating money. No matter the duration of the investment, commercial properties ensure the investor generates a good amount from the property.

Engage the services of a professional company: You will require help, especially in a foreign country. You need to engage the services of a local property investor to assist you with the right kind of services. There may be a large number of fraudulent individuals who would be ever ready to swindle you of your money because they understand you do not know anything about the operations in the country. There are countries that do not encourage foreign individuals to own property in their country. So, this would create a problem for investors who are willing to make an investment. The best way to go about it is to make use of a professional service company that would assist in getting the property and protect your interest as the investor.

Financing the property: This is also an important step to consider when looking to buy property in a foreign country. Purchasing a rental property in a foreign country would require a lot of financial commitment. The question is " How prepared are you for this huge step?" It is a huge step that shouldn't be treated with a nonchalant attitude. Another factor to consider is the exchange rate of the country you want to invest in. There are bound to be fluctuations in the exchange rate, and this can take a negative toll on your finances. You must understand that buying a property in a foreign country would require that you convert the required money in the country's currency. A typical example of a country where this is prevalent is in Latin America. In Latin America, the exchange rates can hinder the ability of an investor to purchase properties. The majority of Latin America transactions are usually conducted using US dollars. This is not always the case, as some people still buy properties using cash transactions.

The use of the property: You need to understand what you want to use the property for. There are various ways to make use of the property. There are options at your disposal as an investor. Some of these options include leasing the house on a monthly rent payment or for people who are interested in vacation. However, in doing this, it is pertinent to be cognizant of the regulatory laws that govern rentals and how it operates in the country. There are some countries that place limits on rental conditions. In renting the property for vacation, the competition is usually high, and the potential investors need to be aware of the competitors and the threats it could pose to the intended business.

Maintaining the property: This is a key step that potential investors should be aware of. It is absolutely right for an individual to consider getting a property in a foreign country. But, the main issue lies in the fact that the property owner would not reside in the country where he has acquired a property. Such a property owner may decide to leave the country for different reasons. When the property owner returns to his/ her country of residence, who takes care of the property? How will the issues of repairs and other important factors be taken care of? This issue becomes quite challenging when the property owner cannot speak the language of the immediate environment where he purchased the property. The suitable way of handling this issue is to relate with good neighbors that reside close to your property. You could get them to handle these repairs and maintenance for you, or better still, you can employ the services of a local expat to handle all affairs that may arise in your absence.

Security factors: You are going to leave the property and return to your home of residence, probably in another country. The property will still be in existence even when you are not there to handle it and pay attention to what goes on with it. Natural disasters may likely occur, and you wouldn't want your property to be caught in the middle of it. Political and economic situations can also become a threat to your property. Such a disaster may affect the value of your property and could amount to a huge loss on your part. If the property owner acquired a loan to purchase the rental property, such an investor would definitely incur huge losses. The only option available to the investor is to insure the property, but the question still revolves around the possibility of such property thriving in these natural disaster-prone environments. The insurance can only take care of certain aspects of the property and not all. So, it is important that the investor thoroughly considers the risks of acquiring rental properties before making a choice. The insurance on the property will also not cover various insurances on health and other aspects. Endeavor to ask questions on the security aspect of the country before making the final decisions. Security issues are paramount in any country you hope to make an investment in. It could amount to a complete disaster of your project or help to build the investment properly.

Tax: Can you ever live without paying tax? It is unrealistic to believe you can actually get an investment and avoid paying tax. It is not possible. You will pay your taxes whether you accept the conditions or not. The manner at which you are taxed depends on what is obtainable in the preferred country of your choice. Another factor is the way you make use of the property. The manner in which you use the property also determines how you would pay the tax on the property. There are investors who would prefer to rent out a part of the property and live in a unit. For others, they won't stay on the property but would prefer to rent it out entirely. Whatever option the investor chooses determines his tax rate and how much it would be. Additionally, you will need to learn about the tax laws of the rental property you have acquired. In some countries, the tax rate is separated from the rental income, but in other countries, the tax is withheld from the individual's rental income.

Merits of investing in national and international properties

There are too many advantages to investing in foreign countries. There are also some risks attached to this investment type, but fortunately, the benefits outnumber the risks associated with this investment type. Some of the benefits include:

It is a perfect vacation home: Everyone needs a little bit of rest. As an investor, aside from the financial benefits attached to making an investment in foreign countries, it is a good place for a vacation. It saves the investor the cost of acquiring a place for vacation. Whenever the investor wishes to go on a vacation, the investor simply goes to the foreign country where he has made an investment and makes use of his property as a vacation home.

It saves retirement cost: As an investor, it is safer to go on a retirement plan when you have made some investments in foreign countries. It also reduces the amount of money the investor spends on his/ her cost of living.

Investing in international property broadens the investor's cultural scope: When an investor goes to another country to acquire property, the investor interacts with a different culture that is entirely different from what he/she is used to. This helps the investor to gain knowledge of different cultures and improve the investor's cultural experience. Such an investor would be able to see things from a different perspective as a result of interacting with a different type of people.

It improves currency diversity: The investor is not limited to a particular country and their currency values but rather has an idea of the current currency situations of other countries. An investor with a property in a foreign country is not susceptible to the effect of a country's finances. The investor is able to make decisions based on various financial situations because his/ her finances are not tied to only one country. In this way, if anything unfavorable should befall one of the countries, the investor is not affected by it. Also, investing in foreign scenes also protects the investor's currency from devaluation.

It is another source of income from a different country: This does not affect the investor's job or profession in his/ her residential country. It provides a means for the investor to earn money from a different country. A majority of the time, the currency rates of the different countries differ, and it may even be higher. The outstanding part of this benefit is that the investor earns income in a different currency.

Hard assets: There is nothing as promising and fulfilling as knowing that your investment is going to last for a long period of time. The economic situation of different countries is favorable for individuals who possess different investments that can yield income over a long period of time. Owning properties in different countries is secure and assures a more sustainable source of income.

Agricultural benefits: Agriculture is one of the tremendous benefits of having an investment in foreign countries. The populations of different countries are rising by the day, and the means of sustaining the population doesn't equate with the rise in the population. To create this balance, investing in foreign countries is an appropriate strategy.

It is a means of storing wealth: Investing in foreign countries comes with lower entrance cost for some countries. The minimal cost of acquiring property in a foreign country allows room for investors to grow their wealth slowly and steadily. The fact is that, as long as the property is located in a different country, it would reduce the chances of paying money for any issue that arises on your property. A typical example is paying the damages that occurred when an individual got involved in an accident on your property. As long as you are in a distant country, you won't pay the damages fee because it occurred in your absence. More so, you will be saving a good amount of money that would be spent on paying for damages.

The money can then be used for better options. Assets that are in a different country are very difficult to access.

It confers a foreign residence status upon the investor: The chances of owning a resident visa in a country is higher when you have an investment in such a country. The investor is permitted to travel to the country where his asset is located with little or minimal obstruction. You will also be entitled to travel to such a country either for business or tourist reasons.

It helps you improve wealth easily: Making an investment in a foreign country makes it easier for the investors to move his wealth out of his residential country to the country hosting his investment. It makes it difficult for the government or unlawful individuals to have access to your wealth. It is almost impossible or even difficult for the government of a country to confiscate a foreign property. An attempt to do such would bring about a problem or even stir a war. Unlike financial accounts that can be confiscated at any point in time, it is not same for land and landed properties.

Advantage of being internationalized: Having an international property makes it easier for the investor to have a foreign financial account. A foreign property confers one legal access to a country, and such an investor is regarded as a temporary citizen. Additionally, it makes it easier for the investor to have a second citizenship and make use of the country when there are issues with the person's residential home. It offers the investor various opportunities to travel to countries without making use of a visa. There are also rare cases where buying properties in foreign scenes makes it possible for the investor to get immediate citizenship.

It diversifies your portfolio: Investing in materials such as gold, precious stones, and other metals is a good investment but investing in properties in foreign countries is an added advantage. Purchasing lands and homes provides a source of financial security that the other precious materials cannot boast of. More so, income with foreign properties is steady and highly profitable.

Foreign properties maintain a significant level of privacy: Foreign properties are a good way of living a private life and still earning a good source of income. When you invest in foreign countries, a lot of individuals are not aware of your worth. More so, the only permissible way of acquiring the property is in your name and not in the government. Foreign countries are also regarded as the new way of financial banking in the 21st century.

Foreign investment increases your worth: When you make a good investment in foreign countries, it increases your financial worth and positively affects other areas of your life. It further broadens your horizons and helps you to gain the needed insight on how to secure foreign deals and transactions.

The advantages are tremendous and may be regarded as innumerable. The only factor that should be considered by the investor when doing research is the possibility of the investment to generate good returns in time. Additionally, the location of the property should be considered, as well as the time the property is bought. If all these things are in place, then the investor is sure to reap the benefits in the nearest future.

Demerits of investing in national and international properties

Cost of hiring a property manager: Investing in rental properties in a foreign environment presupposes that you will not be available to manage the affairs of your property. Even if you decide to manage your property, it would be done remotely. To ensure property affairs are effectively coordinated, you are left with the option of engaging the services of a property manager, and this, in turn, would be very expensive.

Differences in the currency exchange rate: It is a well-known fact that different countries make use of different currencies. The currency value of one country varies from the next. This can also affect the ability of any investor to make investments in a foreign country. The change in a currency rate cannot be predicted as it fluctuates. When the value of the foreign country's currency is poor, it has an adverse effect on your earnings as an investor. This mitigates the chances of getting huge profits from your investment.

Economic and political changes: The two major factors to look for when attempting to make an investment in a foreign country is the economic and political factors of the supposed country. One thing is certain; both factors are not constant. It is very difficult to predict what happens in a country and when it happens. So, the economic and political change in a country can negatively affect your investment. When the economy of the supposed country is unstable, then your investment becomes unstable as well. In cases of political crisis or conflict, the property would be adversely affected, and this will result in a huge loss on your part as an investor. Whenever you make up your mind to invest in international countries, make sure you have the basic information that surrounds their political and economic factors to prevent circumstances that are beyond your control and that would have an adverse effect on your property.

Inadequate knowledge of the foreign country's laws: This is an aspect of investing in international rental properties that should be taken quite seriously. Failure to acquaint yourself with the right knowledge about the laws that govern the country where you hope to acquire a rental property can cause your plans to shatter. The laws that govern rental properties differ from one country to the next. So, it is important that you have the right information about the foreign country's laws or employ the services of a property manager who would assist you with the appropriate services.

*****

CONCLUSION

Investing in a rental property is always good business. The importance of such an investment can never be underestimated. There is nothing wrong with starting your business venture on a small scale. The rental property will grow when you begin the right way. This is especially true for first- time investors who do not have the right understanding of how to go through the processes involved in owning a rental property. While it is a good idea to start small, it is also a wise decision to consider the amount of finance you have budgeted for such a project.

There are a number of ways to finance your rental property. It can be financed through the use of a mortgage, government loans, the seller's financing, and a host of many other ways. In financing your rental investment, you need to take cognizance of a lot of other factors that can disrupt the whole process. It is not just about financing the project; you also need to understand if the project will be a profitable venture for you.

Information is power. So, you need to seek help from the right source. Don't undermine the importance of getting help from an experienced individual who had better ideas on how to go about real estate properties. You can also choose to belong to a local association where you would get the right kind of help. Carry out a background check on the property you want to purchase. It is also possible that the rental property has existing tenants. You need to understand how to handle such a project. Manage your communication effectively with neighbors and those around you. You can learn from the experiences of others and know the right way to handle your rental property.

You can never do it all alone. You still require the assistance of a professional to handle all matters related to the property. A professional property inspector is all you need to do the inspection of your property. The property inspector helps you to detect every fault or hidden problem in the property. Such an inspection also ensures that the property owner is aware of the condition of the property before purchasing it. Also, it provides the investor with a number of options to choose from. The investor can choose either to take up the rental property or make the appropriate repairs on the property. In cases where the investor feels that the repairs are too much for him to handle, such an investor can settle for a rent-ready apartment that would make it easier for him to earn money. The advantage of the rent-ready apartment is that it helps the investor make money from the property, and it is the easiest way to begin an investment.

The economy and rental value of the property are also very important to put under consideration. In purchasing the property, you need to know the worth of the property you intend to purchase. Understand how economy cycles would likely affect the rental property. More so, get an in-depth understanding of how much the renters are willing to pay for rent on the property. The place of unemployment and inflation must be adequately understood, and the manner the factors can affect the rental property. The rental property you hope to purchase can also cost you a fortune for maintenance and other related needs. The understanding of how rent fluctuates with the economic situation of an environment affects the state of the property. Every investor needs to come to the realities of the factors that may affect their investment in the long run. The major economic factors are inflation and unemployment. Though, the right kind of rental property will ensure that you do not get totally affected by these economic factors.

Advertising your rental property is a good strategy to attract the right kind of tenants for your property. To avoid a situation where just any kind of renter comes to rent your property, make sure you specifically state the type of renters you desire on your property. This would make it easier for the right kind of tenants to rent your property. Also, make use of appropriate advertising channels to reach the right kind of tenants.

The type of renters that you permit to stay on your property is also very necessary to avoid a situation where the investor makes a wrong choice in selecting renters. The type of rental property you invest in should be designed to meet the ideal renters you hope to attract on your property. Get suitable amenities that your ideal renters will appreciate. Provide the necessary amenities close to your rental property to aid your target renters to have the right access to the various amenities.

The best way to protect your investment is by having the right kind of documents to back up your claims. This implies that, when you get a rental property, you must be in possession of an agreement that would be legally binding between you and the tenants, as well as your property manager. The reason for this is to prevent any chances of having controversial issues stem from the claims of your property. It is always good to specify the rules and regulations that state the conditions of living on your property. Having tenants on your property comes with a lot of responsibilities, and this can turn out to be bad for the investor. An investor may lose all that he has worked for by making a mistake in protecting his investment. The only way to protect the investment is by ensuring there would be the presence of certain documents that would be duly signed by the tenants and the property owner.

Aside from investing in residence homes, investing in vacation properties is also a profitable venture. It is even more lucrative in situations where the cost of the property is cheaper and when the residents are willing to pay for the services of the vacation property. Get the services of a property manager to manage the property for you. Ensure you research the vacation home you intend to purchase. This would save you from a whole lot of trouble that can negatively affect your finances.

Another way of investing in rental property is to invest in international scenes. Investing in a foreign country is very profitable for the investor. It enables the investor to earn income in a foreign currency, learn about different cultures, as well as manage his finances accordingly. Although there are disadvantages attached to such investment, the benefits outnumber the disadvantages.

Rental property investing is a good source of making passive income and helps the investor make the right kind of choice that would affect his source of income.

www.ingramcontent.com/pod-product-compliance
Lightning Source LLC
Chambersburg PA
CBHW070636220526
45466CB00001B/190